C000218772

How to Develop and Present Staff Training Courses

How to Develop and Present Staff Training Courses

SECOND EDITION

Peter Sheal

Kogan Page Ltd, London
Nichols Publishing Company,
New Jersey

First published in 1989
This second edition published in 1994
Reprinted 1997

Apart from any fair dealing for the purposes of research or private study, or criticism
or review, as permitted under the Copyright, Designs and Patents Act, 1988, this
publication may only be reproduced, stored or transmitted, in any form or by any
means, with the prior permission in writing of the publishers, or in the case of
reprographic reproduction in accordance with the terms of licences issued by the
Copyright Licensing Agency. Enquiries concerning reproduction outside those terms
should be sent to the publishers at the undermentioned address:

Kogan Page Limited
120 Pentonville Road
London N1 9JN

© Peter Sheal, 1989, 1994

British Library Cataloguing in Publication Data

A CIP record for this book is available from the British Library

ISBN (UK) 0 7494 1231 3
ISBN (US) 0 89397 439 0

Published in the USA by Nichols Publishing
PO Box 6036, East Brunswick, New Jersey 08816
Typeset by Books Unlimited (Nottm), Rainworth, NG21 0JE
Printed and bound in Great Britain by Biddles Ltd, Guildford and King's Lynn

Contents

Preface

Since the first edition of this book was published in 1989 there have been many new developments in training and the trainer's role in organizations has expanded. In addition to the traditional role of developing and conducting training courses, trainers are increasingly responsible for improving job performance, for employee development generally, and implementing change in organizations.

This expansion of the trainer's role together with improvements in training technology have led me to include in this second edition additional material on:

- learning in the organization
- competence-based training
- job observation and task analysis
- producing training videos
- workplace assessment.

Courses in training and development sponsored by the Institute of Training and Development (now the Institute of Personnel Development) have also increased in popularity over the past few years. In response, I have geared this book more closely to the needs of students. In particular, the Action Items at the end of each chapter are designed to help them develop their in-company projects.

As trainers we have always focused on making our training more effective – improving our presentations, producing better visuals, using more interesting exercises. These activities were amply dealt with in the first edition of this book, but I have updated information and added more examples and training tools where these might prove helpful. The key to improved training results, however, lies in increasing the involvement of participants and ensuring that their organizations are fully committed to the success of the training. These are areas where significant improvements can be made and which I have re-emphasized in this second edition.

Peter Sheal
Spring 1994

Acknowledgements

Thanks to my son, David Sheal, for his information and experience of workplace assessment, to Gene Fitzpatrick for his comments on video production, and to Michel Bekhazi for his input on training techniques.

Introduction

Training was once the poor relation of education. Training was something for the youngsters who had been unsuccessful at school, and trainers were industrial teachers but without the status of degrees and qualifications after their names. Rapid technological advances, changes in the patterns of employment, and the unemployment of the 1980s and 1990s have changed all that however. The high-flown phrases about 'investing in people' and people being 'our most valuable resource' have become business reality. There are four main reasons why staff training and development have become more important:

- rapid changes in technology and the jobs people do
- immediate and long-term skills shortages
- changes in the composition and expectations of the workforce
- competition and market pressures for improvements in the quality of products and services.

Rapid changes in technology and the jobs people do. With accelerating changes in technology and work systems, many traditional industrial and clerical jobs have changed radically or become obsolete. New jobs have been created, particularly in the service and information-based industries. According to the US Labor Department, the average American entering the workforce today will change careers at least three times during his working life. A similar situation applies to European workers, who are now facing the increased labour mobility and skill demands generated by the Single Market. In order to cope with these changes people need 'portable skills' that will keep them employable when their current jobs change or vanish.

In some cases people may have the skills and experience to do a specific job when they are recruited. Increasingly however employers are recruiting young people who have the 'basics' or the 'potential' to do a job and then training them on the job. Then as the work environment and the job change, employees are expected to update their skills. If they don't have opportunities for training, retraining and development, then, they and their skills can become 'obsolete'.

Immediate and long-term skills shortages. Technological developments have led to a higher percentage of skill- and knowledge-based jobs and a greater demand for skilled workers – and a decreased requirement for unskilled labour. This is a problem particularly for countries like the UK which have more unskilled than skilled workers. Even when unemployment has been high in the UK, there have been skills shortages, limiting business expansion and the use of new technology and production techniques.

Over the longer term, such skills shortages are expected to increase through the greater complexity of jobs and the decreasing numbers of young people entering the workforce. In the West the 'baby boom' generation of the post- Second World War period has become the mature employees of the 1980s and 90s. They will reach pensionable age in the early part of the next century when the ' baby bust' of the 1960s and 70s will lead to a reduction in the working population.

Again this skills gap can only be overcome by an expansion of training, retraining and staff development opportunities. Workers can then move more easily from the unskilled to the skilled labour market, thereby reducing skills shortages and the pool of long-term unemployed and unskilled labour.

Changes in the composition and expectations of the workforce. In the past people expected their education and training to last them a lifetime. Now full-time schooling is recognized as providing only basic foundations for a person's working life. In particular, the increasing proportion of managerial, supervisory, and professional workers in the workforce has led to a greater demand for professional development opportunities. This in turn has encouraged a demand from all levels of staff for increased training and development. Nobody wants to become 'obsolete'.

Competition and market pressures for improvements in the quality of products and services. There is an increased recognition that only 'quality people' – managers, supervisors and staff with up-to-date knowledge and expertise – can produce high quality products and services. Many organizations are introducing total quality management and quality assurance programmes which require the cooperation, involvement and retraining of the workforce if they are to be successful. Training and staff development are recognized as primary means for achieving the better quality products and services needed to compete in world markets.

All these factors have led to an increased demand for training. In the United States corporate expenditure on training has risen significantly. A survey by *Training* magazine showed that in 1993 about $48 billion had been budgeted for formal training by those US organizations with one hundred or more employees. This was an increase of 7 per cent over the 1992 budget. *Training* also reported in 1993 that approximately 47 million staff were receiving formal training for an average of four days per year and an average cost of $1,000 per head. A similar increase in expenditure on training has taken place in the UK. In 1993 *Training & Development* magazine reported that the Training and Enterprise Councils had a budget of almost 2 billion. In addition, a survey by the Industrial Society showed that companies spent an average of £492 per employee on training with each employee spending a total of just over four days being trained during the year.

With this rise in expenditure, training has increased in diversity, complexity, and level of sophistication. Training has become more important within organizations and employees are spending an increasing amount of time in training activities. As a consequence, more people are taking on training responsibilities within their organizations and becoming full-time or part-time trainers.

Who are trainers?

When we talk about trainers we are talking about a group of people carrying out a broad range of functions. The actual job title, role and responsibilities of a trainer tend to differ from organization to organization, but among the most common jobs are:

■ *Training officer* – responsible for coordinating a variety of training tasks within a company. Activities may include developing and conducting courses, recruiting contract trainers and consultants to provide internal and external training programmes, and arranging for staff to take courses at local colleges.
■ *Management trainer* – responsible for conducting training courses for supervisors and managers.
■ *Teacher trainer* – responsible for developing the instructional skills of prospective teachers and/or providing in-service training for serving teachers.
■ *Technical trainer* – responsible for the technical training of new employees and more experienced staff. For example, a trainer in a computer centre usually provides training in the use of specific computer hardware and programs.
■ *On-the-job trainer or mentor* – an experienced and skilled employee who provides on-the-job training for inexperienced employees.
■ *Workplace assessor* – a supervisor or skilled craftsman responsible for assessing employees' on-the-job performance.
■ *Instructional designer* – responsible for developing learning materials like booklets, videos and computer-based training, for courses conducted by other trainers or for open learning programmes.

What does a trainer do?

Depending on the situation within an organization, a trainer may perform all or a number of the above functions. What unites these functions, however, is that

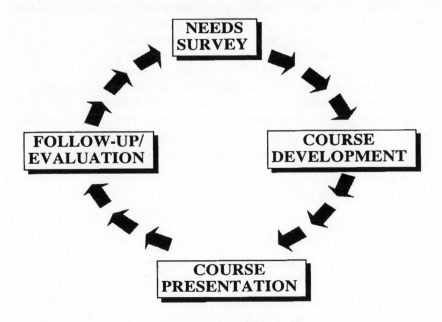

Figure O.1 *The training cycle*

they are all, in some way, involved with helping people to learn and develop. The skills that a trainer needs in order to accomplish this primary objective include:

1. Promoting learning in organizations
2. Identifying training needs
3. Designing training courses
4. Developing training materials
5. Delivering training courses
6. Evaluating the effectiveness of training

This book is concerned with providing information and improving your skills in these areas. The chapters focus on specific training skills and the steps in the training cycle shown in Figure O.1. The chapters are as follows:

Chapter 1: How to promote learning in organizations focuses on the adult learner and how you, the trainer, can promote effective learning among participants in your courses and employees in your organization.
Chapter 2: How to identify staff training needs and involve the client describes how you can use a needs assessment, not only to identify needs but to gather information and support for the development of training programmes.

Chapter 3: How to design a training course for active learning describes how you can design and develop a training course to fit the needs of your organization's staff.

Chapter 4: How to develop and use effective training materials explains how you can develop and use print and audio-visual materials for training courses.

Chapter 5: How to deliver training that engages participants describes some of the methods and techniques you can use to make your training courses or seminars more effective.

Chapter 6: How to evaluate training effectiveness and job performance explains how you can evaluate, follow-up and report on the effectiveness of training courses.

Throughout the text there are job aids or training tools which you might adapt to your own situation and needs. These job aids or training tools are usually completed as examples.

1

How to promote learning in organizations

Training should not be confused with learning. Your organization may be doing a lot of training, but that does not mean people are learning very much. Learners themselves control the switch that makes learning happen. We may call this switch motivation, the need to learn, or the desire for involvement. The trainer's job is to promote learning and to ensure that learners stay 'switched on'.

This chapter describes how people learn and some stages in individual and organizational learning. We will consider ten factors which promote adult learning and discuss the impact of each factor on the development of training. Finally we will look at ways you can use this information when you conduct training sessions and specific methods you can apply to ensure learning.

Training and learning

Over recent years there has been a significant shift in the focus of adult education and training. The emphasis has moved from the teacher or trainer, the transmission of information and how best this can be improved, to a focus on the learner and how best to promote learning. But what is learning and how does it occur?

Mention of the word learning immediately evokes in most people images of school – desks in a row, chalkboard, school bells. As a result, people often confuse teaching or training and learning. In business organizations around the world thousands of employees sit in classrooms, they receive many hours of instruction but the fact that they are sat there and attentive doesn't mean they are learning. They may be wondering when the next break is due, thinking about the work piling up while they are away, planning their evening – their thoughts may be far away from the training course they are attending.

The trainer's primary function is to help people learn and develop; in order to promote learning, however, you need to know something about how people learn and how they learn best. Below are two definitions of learning. Which of these definitions best fits your own view of learning?

1. A collection of facts and ideas that people gain at school and keep adding to throughout their lives.

This is a school-based and static definition of learning, an Encyclopaedia Britannica view. It supports the belief of some people that they have largely completed their learning: they already have a 'full set' from their days at school and just keep adding extra volumes with each passing year.

2. A mental or physical process leading to changes in behaviour.

This is a more dynamic view of learning and involves learning on the job and through life. This view fits in with current research on intelligence which demonstrates that intelligence is not a static element but an open dynamic system that can continue to develop through life. It also emphasizes that most of the significant learning in our lives comes from what we do – that learning is not something separate from life, but is gained through action. This definition of learning is also linked to changes in behaviour, to continuous improvement, and is the one adopted in this book.

Researchers tend to agree that learning involves:

■ An active rather than a passive process. Few people now think of learning as 'receiving instruction'. Instead learning is increasingly defined as an activity in which learners participate and are actively involved.

■ A relatively permanent change in behaviour. The change may be, and often is, an increased capability for some kind of performance. It may also involve a change in attitude or interest.

■ The acquisition of additional information, skills or attitudes. Learning then may be simply an addition to what you know or can do already – your present knowledge, skills, or attitude + X. Learning, however, may also be a subtraction like unlearning a bad or ineffective habit – stopping smoking or reducing the number of hestitations when you speak in public. Learning may also be a modification where old knowledge, skills, or attitudes are adjusted to cope with new circumstances.

Learning may be conscious or unconscious but everything we want to learn, everything we want to embed in our long-term memory, must always take the same route: from ultra short-term memory, to short-term memory, and then to long-term memory. Learning, this transfer of information from the short-term to the long-term memory, is speeded up when:

■ The same information or practice is repeated several times. Repetition sets the ultra short-term/short-term/long-term memory mechanism in motion. In training this highlights the importance of periodic review and practice.

■ The new information is associated with some information or a picture already in the long-term memory. This emphasizes the need for the trainer to link new information or ideas with what learners already know.

■ The brain is allowed to pause and no new information is transmitted to it. This emphasizes that trainers need to provide time for learners to assimilate new information and apply it, or to practise any new skills they have learned.

■ The movement of electrical impulses is speeded up by what might be called joyful stress. People learn more quickly when they enjoy a training session.

The transfer of information to long-term memory and therefore learning can be slowed or blocked when:

■ Too much, or confusing, information has to be assimilated in too short a time. Training sessions which focus on providing as much information as possible in the shortest amount of time are rarely effective.

■ The learner experiences distress or shock eg, panic during an exam. Such distress or shock blocks the electrical impulses to the long-term memory. This emphasizes that in situations which are potentially threatening eg, a role-play, a videotaped presentation or a performance test, the trainer should do everything possible to make the participants feel at ease.

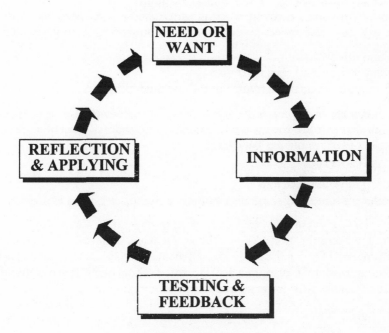

Figure 1.1 *Wheel of learning*

How people learn

It is interesting to note how many processes within individuals and in organizations are described in cycles. In the introduction to this book we looked at the training cycle in Figure 0.1. In the recent research and literature, learning too is often represented as a cyclical process: in concrete terms as a wheel of learning, as shown in Figure 1.1. There are many versions of this learning cycle but all recognize that learning is a continuous process and involves action and reflection. The wheel describes the four stages in the learning process and we will look at each stage in detail with some examples.

The first stage is *wanting* or *needing* to learn. Essentially people learn what they want to learn. They may want to succeed in something, find the answer to a question or problem. For example:

■ I want to drive
■ I want to qualify for this job
■ I want to learn how to use this computer program.

The second stage is *information gathering*. The information may be gained through formal instruction or informal learning. *Formal instruction* is provided at school, through courses, etc. We all know about formal instruction but often do not pay much attention to, or are particularly conscious of *informal learning*. This involves taking advantage of learning opportunities – at work and home. For example, by reading something, working with someone else, asking for advice or input on a particular project. Examples of the information-gathering stage are:

■ Taking driving lessons
■ Taking a vocational training course
■ Reading the manual and trying out the computer program.

The third stage in the learning cycle is *testing and feedback*. This may involve feedback arising from when you try things out and feedback from other people. Examples of testing and feedback are:

■ Taking the driving test
■ Taking the vocational tests
■ Producing something using the computer program.

Stage 4 is *reflection and applying*. This involves applying the information you have gathered to more situations. You might sit down and evaluate the results of the test, the results of trying the thing out, and mentally apply what you have learned to other situations. If learning a skill is involved, you might practise that skill further or transfer that skill to other situations. For example:

■ Driving by yourself
■ Practising your trade
■ Using the computer program to work on a new project.

Most important of all, application involves asking ourselves the questions – *What did I learn? How can I apply it to other situations?*

In some situations the cycle may be followed sequentially; more often the stages overlap. For example, it's important to continue wanting while doing. Many people drop out of formal learning courses because they lose the initial motivation. Many people stop learning new things because of a lack of need – they are comfortable with what they have already learned.

Adult learning: ten principles

We can see that learning takes place more readily in some circumstances than in others. Education and training are planned learning and based on what we know from learning theory and experience. Here is a list of ten factors which promote adult learning and the likelihood that training will be successful. Obviously these factors are linked – indeed an effective training course and trainer will take account of most, if not all of them – but at the risk of some duplication it's useful to distinguish these points. Adults learn better:

1. When they want or need to learn something – there is the motivation to learn.
2. In comfortable learning environments that foster mutual trust and respect.
3. When their individual learning needs and learning styles are catered for.
4. When their previous knowledge and experience are valued and used.
5. When they have some control over the learning content and activities.
6. When there is a focus on dealing with realistic problems and applying learning.
7. Through active mental and physical participation in learning activities.
8. When sufficient time is provided for learning – the assimilation and application of new information, the practice of new skills, or changes in attitude.
9. When there are opportunities to successfully practise or apply learning.
10. When there are some measures of competence or performance so that people have a sense of progress towards their goals.

Now let us look at each learning factor in turn and consider its impact on the development and delivery of training courses. In particular, let's consider ways in which you can make use of these factors in training sessions and the specific methods you can apply to promote learning.

1. Motivation to learn

Adults may be motivated to learn something for a variety of reasons: a change in their lives or their jobs; a desire for job advancement; a love of learning or the desire to do something new. In some cases the learner may be sufficiently motivated to overcome every obstacle put up by poor facilities, a boring trainer and a badly planned course. In the majority of cases however, the initial need and desire to learn must be enhanced and sustained if the learner is successfully to complete the training. In most cases, the trainer's handling of the course and interaction with the learners makes all the difference between success and failure.

Trainers often ask themselves, 'What can I do to motivate my learners and keep them motivated?'. Although they always agree on the importance of motivation, trainers rarely agree on what best motivates learners. The following is a brief survey of some of the most relevant research on motivation and of its implications for training.

Maslow's hierarchy of human needs

One of the most significant theories of motivation is AH Maslow's hierarchy of human needs. Based on his psychological research and observations, Maslow proposed that individuals try to satisfy the following needs (see Figure 1.2):

Physiological or survival needs. These are the most basic needs and include the needs for food, water and warmth. If learners lack these basics, then training should focus on helping them to satisfy these needs – for example basic training in farming, irrigation and other survival skills.
Safety needs. These involve living in a safe and secure physical and emotional environment. This second level is relevant to training, particularly if learners have been away from education or training for a long time. Learners may feel vulner-

Figure 1.2 *Maslow's hierarchy of human needs*

able – afraid they will not fit in with the others, afraid they may make mistakes or make fools of themselves. The trainer here needs to provide a safe and secure emotional environment.

Need for love, affection and a sense of belonging. This involves the desire to be accepted and to develop friendships. Reference to this level shows why it is particularly important for learners to feel at ease and part of the group at the beginning of a training session. Then they can start to learn.

Need for esteem. This involves the desire to have a positive image of yourself, and to receive recognition, attention and appreciation from others for your contributions. Clearly the need for esteem and fear of losing esteem play an important part in training.

Need for self-actualization. Maslow states that this is the highest need category. Here the individual is concerned with developing to his or her full potential as an individual. The chance to be creative and autonomous is important not only as a job motivator, but in training. Creative exercises, individual learning projects and self-managed learning are means of harnessing this need for self-actualization.

Based on this hierarchy, Maslow proposed that satisfaction of the needs on each level, starting with the lowest, freed a person for higher levels of satisfaction. In other words, when someone has satisfied levels 1, 2 and 3 then they can go on to learn for esteem, individual achievement and self-development purposes. Training courses and trainers should therefore attempt to satisfy those upper level needs.

Keller's ARCS model

Over recent years John Keller's work on motivation has gained a wide audience in the training and development field. Keller has put forward the ARCS model for producing more stimulating training materials and for conducting more motivating training sessions. The ARCS model consists of the following elements:

Attention. The first requirement in any training course is to gain your learners' attention. Interest or curiosity must be aroused and maintained.

Relevance. The learners have to see something of relevance in the training. In other words, the instruction must have some personal value, job relevance, or importance to them.

Confidence. Motivation to learn is increased by confidence. Learners must believe that they can accomplish the goals and be successful. Research has shown that learners are highly motivated in courses where there are early 'opportunities for success' and they can develop confidence. If our early experience of learning something makes us feel 'I'm good at this!', we are likely to become successful.

Satisfaction. Learners may receive external rewards eg, certificates, awards etc., but internal satisfactions are more important. Learners will be motivated towards further learning if they gain satisfaction from a training session and feel they have really learned something.

Training applications

Your attitude as a trainer, in particular your enthusiasm, is a key factor in motivating learners. Perhaps the most powerful way of conveying enthusiasm is through your tone of voice, your eyes, gestures and other body language. If you, the trainer, are not motivated and enthusiastic, you cannot expect learners to be. Indeed they are quick to detect a lack of interest on the part of the trainer and will often lose interest soon after you do.

Your enthusiasm should not only be for the course content however; in your responses and work with individuals you show whether you are interested in the learners or not. When you notice that interest is flagging, you should examine yourself rather than the participants. When people look bored, check your own presentation, the clock (you may have talked for too long), or the level of people's involvement in an activity. You might change your approach, move to another activity, give a short break, or encourage participation through questions or a discussion. The effective trainer does not just plod along, thinking that these 'ungrateful' participants *should* be more interested.

Here are a few examples of how Maslow's work on motivation can lead us to use specific training techniques:

■ We should think of ways in which learners can satisfy their need for esteem in the training situation. These might include learners contributing to discussions, producing something, demonstrating a skill, or working as members of a team.

■ Most adult learners are mature people and are mainly motivated by the upper-level needs. If problems occur in the training however, a learner may step back to a lower level of needs. For example, if the learner feels threatened in a training activity, safety and belongingness needs may temporarily come to the fore. You will need to satisfy this desire for security to avoid the learner becoming demotivated and to encourage him or her to focus on the satisfaction of higher level learning needs.

Here are a few examples of how Keller's model can lead us to use specific training techniques:

■ *Attention*
  - Start with questions and use varied questioning techniques to maintain attention.
  - Capture participants' attention through an introductory activity that gets them involved.
  - Vary the methods and pace of the training activities.
  - Use attention-grabbing visual aids eg, video, slides, or overhead transparencies.
■ *Relevance*
  - Provide information or elicit answers from the participants so that they know, 'What's in it for me?'

- Relate the course to learners' needs/wants and present or future goals.
- Refer to, and use, learners' previous knowledge and experience.
- Use job simulations and authentic activities eg, case studies, role plays, team assignments.
- Show how the information and skills gained through training can be used on or off the job.
■ *Confidence*
  - Ensure that the learning aims or objectives are achievable.
  - Provide opportunities for successful practice early in the course.
  - Behave as if participants are certain to learn.
■ *Satisfaction*
  - Provide opportunities for learners to show their skills or products.
  - Reinforce success through praise.
  - Provide external rewards and recognition eg, certificates, awards.
  - Reinforce participants' satisfaction at having completed the training successfully.

Reinforcement through the use of praise is a particularly effective motivator. A learning session which does not include reinforcement ie, a good and timely dose of praise, may not bring about the desired change in behaviour. You should give a lot of praise at the beginning of a new and difficult subject or with a new and inexperienced participant. This ties in with opportunities for early success. Then reinforcement should become rarer as learners master the subject area or skill and become more experienced.

Because each person is different, with unique qualities, experience levels, needs and desires, each will be motivated differently. Some will be motivated entirely through relevance and by knowing 'What's in it for me?'. Others need a complex array of motivators. Some people will arrive at the training session highly motivated and require little stimulus from the trainer. Others will arrive with little or no interest and will have to be stimulated by the trainer or the course if they are going to learn. You can find more information on the motivational factors in course development in Chapter 3 and the motivational aspects of course presentation are discussed in Chapter 5.

2. Comfortable learning environments

For many adults training can seem a rather strange and somewhat fearful experience. They feel they are going back to school again, with all the associations of dependence and perhaps unpleasantness that this evokes. They may remember the traditional school atmosphere of formality, semi-anonymity, and distance between teacher and student. They may remember physical and mental punishment.

As we have seen, fear is the greatest enemy of learning, first of all, because it demotivates learners and secondly because it causes a mental block in the brain.

Among the fears and anxieties that learners sometimes bring with them to the training session are:

■ Fear of the trainer who might expose them in some way.
■ Fear of other group members who could laugh at mistakes and thus diminish the learner's self-esteem.
■ Fear of failure, of not performing well and the possible consequences of this for the learner's career.

As a trainer therefore, you must do all you can to create an atmosphere which is free of fear and anxiety, and in which participants are physically and psychologically comfortable. In order to overcome any 'negative associations' or feelings you should provide a friendly informal atmosphere where participants are known by their first name and valued as individuals with something to contribute.

Training applications

The verbal and non-verbal communication (body language) between the trainer and participants at the beginning of a course helps to establish the 'learning climate'. Psychologists have found that every type of communication has two aspects: the communication's content and the relationship between the communicators. Every contact between two human beings therefore takes place simultaneously on two levels: on an intellectual level, which involves information, and on an emotional level, which involves feelings and the relationship between the two people. According to psychologists the emotional level is the more important of the two and particularly when people have only just met, relationship *determines* content. In a training context this means that the trainer operates at two levels:

■ The task level concerned with the transfer of information or skills and the achievement of objectives.
■ The process or relationship level concerned with ensuring that people work easily with each other, participants receive individual attention, and that conflict does not disrupt the group.

In order to establish a comfortable and harmonious climate at the beginning of a course therefore, you should focus on the relationship level before moving onto the task level.

The arrangement of the training room in particular contributes to the 'learning climate'. You should avoid setting up the training room in ways that are reminiscent of school and try instead to provide physical conditions that are comfortable and encourage interaction among participants. Tables and chairs should be arranged so as to allow people to work closely together in pairs or groups and take part in open discussions (for more information on room set-up see Chapter 5).

If participants are to feel at ease, they need to know how they'll 'fit in', what topics will be dealt with and what they should be able to do by the end of the course. They also need to know what activities they'll be involved in – group discussion, role plays, listening to presentations, etc. When you provide participants with this information at the beginning of the course, it eliminates uncertainty and calms fears. Participants know what to expect and that there will be no unpleasant surprises such as a test or evaluation they had not anticipated.

You can also reduce anxiety by starting from the familiar and the known and then proceeding to the unfamiliar and the unknown. This means that you should first find out what the participants already know, then link what they know with what they are about to learn.

Another way in which you can help participants overcome any feelings of isolation and anxiety is to help them identify with the group. When you provide early and active involvement with the rest of the group, for example in an introductions exercise, this helps participants meet many of their 'social needs'. Later group activities should also help build up and maintain friendly relationships among the learners.

Learner anxieties sometimes arise during practice activities, role-plays, demonstrations, or group exercises. You should try to ensure that individual members receive mostly positive feedback from the group. However, when an individual's effort is not acknowledged or when criticism of an individual is too strong to be constructive, you can compensate by identifying and praising the participant's contribution or strengths.

During the training session you should reduce any threat to the participant's ego or self-esteem in front of his or her peers. Particularly at the beginning of a session, there should be opportunities for successful participation and practice. Success is a powerful incentive and throughout the course you should try to reduce the risks of failure.

3. Individual learning needs and styles

Not everyone needs to learn something for the same reasons. One person attending an instructional skills course may need to teach formal classes, another may train groups in a workshop, another may train in one-to-one situations in a plant. In a supervisory skills course you may have a similar mix of participants: a group of young people who are being groomed for promotion, a group who have been supervisors for some time, and then a group of experienced supervisors coming along for a 'refresher'. Again these individuals and groups will differ in their interests and needs.

Just as learners have their own individual needs, so they have their own preferred style of learning. Worlds are created by brains, and the way in which we experience the world and experience training is fundamentally affected by which hemisphere of our brain is dominant. Figure 1.3 indicates the characteristics associated with each hemisphere of the brain.

The logical, rational, sequential analysis of information that we call 'thinking' is associated with the left hemisphere. The making of associations, insights that produce a new 'big picture', and the free flow of creative ideas are associated with

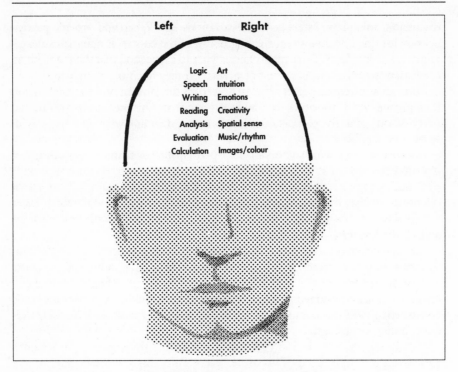

Figure 1.3 *Hemispheres of the brain*

the right hemisphere. Experiments have shown that people who tend to use or have been trained to use one side of the brain more than the other (accountants and engineers, vs artists and musicians) find it difficult to 'switch' when necessary. However, when the weaker side of the brain is stimulated and encouraged to cooperate with the stronger side there is a great increase in ability and effectiveness. Clearly trainers and training courses should provide activities that encourage learners to use both hemispheres of the brain. By engaging in activities that require an alternative way of handling information, participants can gain new perspectives.

Within a particular group of learners there is also likely to be a variety of preferred learning styles. These not only affect how people learn in educational and training situations, but also influence their decision making, problem solving and lifestyle in general. David A Kolb identified four important dimensions of learning style – *reflective observation, abstract conceptualization, active experimentation* and *concrete experience*.

Reflective observation is the preferred style of those learners who rely heavily on and learn best from situations that allow for careful, impartial observation. The key word for this style is 'watching'.

Abstract conceptualization is the preferred style of those who have an analytical and conceptual approach to learning and rely heavily on logical thinking and rational evaluation. These learners prefer to learn from theory, from impersonal situations, and to integrate new learning with what is already known. The key word for this style is 'thinking'. This style tends to be preferred by those who have been successful in maths or science at school.

Active experimentation which involves trial and error discovery methods is often preferred by learners with mechanical and scientific interests – people who like to tinker about with electrical equipment or cars. The active experimenter takes a pragmatic approach to learning and is always asking, 'Yes, but will it work?'. The key word for these learners is 'doing'.

Concrete experience is the preferred style of learners who have an experience-based approach to learning. They learn best from specific examples, involvement and discussions and tend to have a distaste for generalization and abstraction. The key word here is 'feeling'.

Training applications

You need to provide a variety of activities and vary your training methods to cater for participants' differing learning needs. You may need to adapt your materials to fit the different groups and customize the training through individual and group tasks. These may include the completion of participant questionnaires, the development of individual action plans, work on job-related projects or learning journals.

In the same way you need to vary your activities and methods to cater for differing learning styles. *Reflective observers* tend to find lectures or formal presentations useful and consider they help them to learn. A group of teachers with a humanities background are likely to include a large number of participants who tend towards *reflective observation*. They will be more tolerant of formal presentations and generally enjoy activities which involve theoretical discussion. *Abstract conceptualizers* on the other hand tend to learn best from case studies, theoretical readings, graphs and reports.

Active experimenters prefer to learn from projects, practice and feedback from other participants. If you conduct a course for a group of technicians or craftsmen, there are likely to be a large number of *active experimenters*. They will tend to be bored by formal presentations and to become impatient with concepts and abstractions. Learners whose predominant style is *concrete experience* also tend to find theoretical readings and lectures unhelpful. They prefer interpersonal activities like group exercises, discussion and feedback from other learners.

4. Previous knowledge and experience

The differences in knowledge and experience between children and adults have at least three consequences for learning:

- Adults have more to contribute to each other's learning; for most kinds of learning adults are themselves a rich resource.
- Adults have a richer foundation of knowledge and experience to which to relate new information. New learning tends to take on more meaning as adults are able to relate it to their past experience. Indeed, memory is a process which is based on linking and association, and the fewer items there are in the 'recall store', the less the opportunity for new items to be registered and connected.
- Adults have acquired a larger number of fixed habits and patterns of thought and therefore tend to be less open-minded than young people.

Training applications

Adults do not come along to a training session with a blank slate. You should recognize and respect their previous knowledge and experience, and during a training session make as many associations as possible with information already stored in the memory. Build on what learners already know, working from the known to the unknown, and increase their chances of effective learning. Malcolm Knowles (1980), one of the 'fathers' of adult education, writes:

Adults are what they have done. Because adults define themselves largely by their experience, they have a deep investment in its value. And so when they find themselves in situations in which their experience is not being used, or its worth is minimized, it is not just their experience that is being rejected – they feel rejected as persons.

If you ignore adults' previous knowledge and experience, they may insist on the legitimacy of their previous knowledge and close their minds. This is one of the major problems when you are introducing new ideas or methods. You need to recognize and not be negative about the old way of doing things unless the participants are. In most situations you can argue that changed circumstances require the new approach or methods.

Keller's ARCS model factors – Attention, Relevance, Confidence, Satisfaction – are all enhanced if you use and build on people's previous knowledge and experience. They often pay more attention to, and feel more confident about, something that is related to their prior knowledge and experience. They feel satisfied with something that adds to what they already know or can do – in particular, they feel satisfied that they are progressing.

One way of harnessing people's previous experience and making training more relevant is to ask them to bring along problem situations, or to elicit these situations at the beginning of a training course. In this way you can help learners to apply their new knowledge or skills to their experience and make the learning more meaningful.

You should also adjust your presentation and materials to the learners' levels of knowledge and experience. You can find out these levels through a needs survey carried out before the course is presented. If that is not possible, this information can be elicited through an introductory activity at the beginning of the course.

Because adults know more and have experienced more, participatory techniques like discussion, case studies, role-plays and group tasks can be highly effective. Participants learn through exchanging information and previous experience with each other.

In recent years the need to appreciate and give credit for what people already know or can do, their prior knowledge and previous experience, has been recognized through the concept of *Accredited Prior Learning* (APL). For example, grades of membership in professional bodies are often related to years of experience in the field.

5. Control over learning content and activities

People are happier and work better when they have some control over their working environment. Similarly adults tend to learn more and are more involved when they have some control over the training content and activities. Malcolm Knowles (1980) comments:

The main thrust of modern adult-educational technology is in the direction of inventing techniques for involving adults in ever-deeper processes of self-diagnosis of their own needs for continued learning, in formulating their own objectives for learning, in sharing responsibility for designing and carrying out their learning activities, and in evaluating their progress toward their objectives.

During the 1980s and 1990s, there has been a growing interest in self-directed or self-managed learning. In the business world change is occurring so quickly that there is less time to train people formally – often training can't wait for a course to be developed or classes to be formed. There is a growing awareness that people need to be able to take the initiative and manage their own learning. Consequently there has been an increased interest in self-managed learning, on-the-job training, and the establishment of learning centres where employees can learn in their own time and at their own pace. This approach fits in with the concept of learning through life and of Continuing Professional Development (CPD). The responsibility is placed on the employee to manage his or her own continued learning and professional updating with perhaps some help from other staff or the employer.

Training applications
Adult learners can be involved in the diagnosis of their own needs. Questionnaires or pre-tests can be used at the beginning of a course so that learners can assess their present knowledge, skills or attitudes in a particular area eg, communication skills, cultural awareness, or supervisory style. In this way they can experience dissatisfaction with their current situation and develop a willingness to change.

Learners can exercise more control over the content of the training by providing problem situations, identifying difficulties, or specifying their expectations or needs.

A model of the competences or characteristics required to achieve an ideal performance can be developed through a course or presented by the trainer. For example the characteristics of a good supervisor, a good speaker, a good salesman, a good trainer can be described and discussed. Learners can then measure the gaps between their present competences and those required by the model, standard, or ideal performance. Their consequent dissatisfaction with present inadequacies, linked with a clear sense of direction for self-improvement, is in fact a good definition of the 'motivation to learn'.

It is often useful for adult learners to evaluate themselves. People do not argue with their own data. Through the use of video, questionnaires and other feedback methods you can help participants acquire evidence for themselves about where they are and what progress they are making towards the desired goals.

Learners can also develop their own self-evaluation procedures. For example, a test based on the training might be developed by the learners at the end of a course. Each person or group produces several items for the test and submits them to the trainer who standardizes the test and administers it to all the participants. Another example of self-evaluation is where learners might develop their own presentation checklist for a course which deals with presentation techniques.

6. Focus on dealing with realistic problems and applying learning

Education and school tend to focus on the learning of knowledge and skills that will be used at some time in the distant future. Children are told, 'You'll need this for the exams' or 'This will help you to get a job'. For most adults though, learning is not its own reward – it is a means to an end, not an end in itself. Compared to children, adults are less subject- or information-centred and more problem- or performance-centred. They are usually concerned with learning how to deal with problems that they are faced with now and want fairly immediate solutions.

Training applications

Forge as close a link as possible between the training and the work actually to be performed. A needs survey should establish this link at the beginning and a follow-up after the course should ensure that training is transferred to the job.

Training courses should deal with specific problem areas related to a topic rather than try to deal comprehensively with a whole subject. Instead of general courses on communication, courses like 'Business writing skills' or 'Effective speaking' are more attractive to adults.

One of the most appropriate starting points for a training session is the problems and concerns that participants have on their minds as they enter the session. You can, through some pre-training contact (a letter or telephone call), ask them to bring along their problems or concerns to the training course. Alternatively, you can elicit them at the beginning of the course. Using this approach, an induction course would not focus on the history of the company, but on questions of real-life adjustment and survival. The company's history might well be dealt with during the course but the main objective would be to deal with participants' immediate adjustment and survival concerns. If you do present 'background' *nice-to-know* material, however, try to demonstrate the connection between this material and solid, usable job or personal applications.

Build into the design and development of your course provision for the learners to plan and even rehearse how they are going to apply the new knowledge and skills to their day-to-day lives. At various points, participants might plan, write about, discuss, demonstrate or make presentations on how what they have learned might be applied back on the job. In this way you can gain participant commitment to the application of their learning once they return to the work site.

7. Mental and physical participation

Involvement is the key to learning and people learn more from being 'players' rather than 'spectators' in a training course. This is particularly true when a skill is being learned. If you fail to call on the learner to respond actively, there will be few opportunities to check the effectiveness of learning and provide feedback for reinforcement.

Training applications

Alternate information-giving techniques with more participatory techniques. You can encourage:

- Oral participation through questioning, discussions, participant presentations and reporting sessions.
- Written participation through quizzes, the completion of worksheets, or participants using the flipchart to report on an activity.
- Group activity through group discussions, games, case studies and team projects.
- Physical activity through demonstrations, practices on equipment, or the production of training materials.

Participation not only encourages your learners to learn from each other, but takes you off stage. In particular, it allows you to work with individuals, observe groups and assist where necessary.

In order to illustrate the links between learning, the type of activity and the degree of participant involvement I have modified Edgar Dale's well-known cone of experience (1954). Looking at this cone in Figure 1.4, you can see that each division represents a stage between two extremes – between the abstractions of listening or reading about the 'real thing' to the direct experience of 'doing the real thing'. If you move downwards from the pinnacle of the cone, you move in

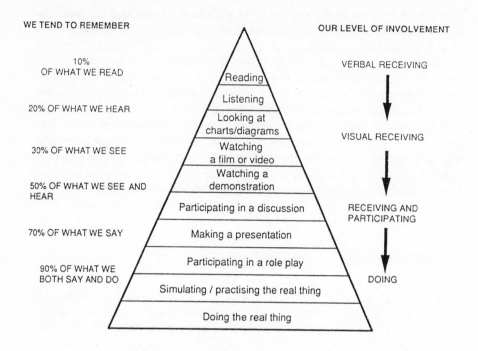

Figure 1.4 *Activity, involvement and learning*

an order of increasing directness, increasing involvement and increased learning. The more senses a learner uses while learning, the faster and more efficiently he or she will remember and learn. Therefore, by appealing to several senses simultaneously the training course and the trainer will increase participant learning.

It's worth noting that training courses in their basic design often follow this downward movement, starting off with fairly passive 'receiving' activities, and culminating in role-play, practice or doing the real thing.

8. Provision of sufficient time for learning.

Research has shown that learning is increased when the brain is allowed to pause and no new additional information is transmitted to it. The recall of information also tends to get progressively worse as time goes on unless the mind is given brief rests. You can promote learning by providing short breaks and time for assimilating the new information or practising the skills already taught.

Understanding and assimilation are also increased when a subject is presented in such a way that its position in the 'big picture' is clear. Connections and cross-references to other relevant areas should be clearly recognizable. This is one reason why an overview at the beginning of a session and a review at the end are so valuable. The more clearly organized the information is and the more connections there are between different parts of a training course, the more effective retention will be; the less structured and coherent the training course, the more easily it will be forgotten.

Training applications
Provide a brief overview at the beginning of a session when you present new information. Then organize the content in such a way that the connections between different parts of the course are clearly visible.

By dividing a major subject area into smaller parts and presenting it over a longer period of time, you can avoid information overload and increase learner assimilation and retention.

When you develop a course and prepare your outline and agenda you need to think of ways to avoid participant fatigue. One way is by alternating topics or training methods. If possible, no single topic should be dealt with *in the same way* for more than 20 minutes. In particular, you should limit the length of presentations. A presentation might be followed by a question and answer session, discussion, or small group activity on the same topic. In this way you can avoid information overload and give participants 'thinking time'.

Another way of reducing fatigue among participants is by providing sufficient breaks. These are particularly useful as relaxation points: they get rid of the muscular and mental tension which inevitably builds up during periods of concentration. When there are no breaks the amount of learning declines substantially. Breaks need not mean participants leaving the room however. They may just consist of a few minutes between activities. Indeed short breaks of a few minutes can raise the performance level throughout the day. Breaks of more than 30 minutes however increase the danger of diminishing motivation and participants losing their concentration.

9. Opportunities to practise or apply learning

Participants need to be able to practise and apply what they have learnt if they are going to remember their training and transfer it to real-life situations, hence the importance of practice and early 'opportunities for success' in Keller's ARCS model. As learners begin to apply and practise what they have heard or seen, they establish more relationships between the parts of the training. They become more involved and can perfect or test their understanding of the information or skill.

There is a need for practice however not only in vocational skills training but also in interpersonal skills training. Changes in behaviour are not brought about by intellectual comprehension alone. A participant who has always behaved in a certain way cannot be made to behave differently without being given the chance of practising the new behaviour. He or she must be able to behave in the new way at least once in order to experience the emotions and the effect personally. That's why learning activities like role play, practice and simulation are so important.

Training can only be effective if new behaviour patterns are learned and practised in *active learning* situations.

Training applications

Provide early opportunities for successful practice. These increase participants' confidence and motivation.

Particularly in skill development the principle of *overlearning*, mastery through repetition, is important. *Overlearning* consolidates new information or skills and offsets the effect of forgetting.

Advertisers recognize the value of repetition and how it can imprint a product on the customer's mind. Repetition is also important in helping learners retain new information and skills. Here are three ways in which you can use repetition effectively without being boring:

■ Repetition with a difference. Here you give the same information but you vary the approach. An example would be the use of a video with a follow-up case study or role play to make the same training points.
■ Repetition through review at the end of a course. Review increases learning and can ensure that new learning is established in the long-term memory.
■ Refresher training whereby you cover the same material at a later date. You need to present the information in a different way however, often in less time and with more challenging practice or exercises.

10. Measures of competence or performance

There are philosophical differences between adult educators and trainers on the amount of guidance learners require and how much measurement of performance is desirable. As an adult educator, Malcolm Knowles (1980) speaks admiringly of humanistic educators like Carl Rogers and Abraham Maslow:

who maintain that most human learning is far too complex to be described by observable, measurable, terminal behaviours. They suggest that objectives might more appropriately specify directions of growth, such as 'to develop increasing self-confidence' or 'to develop broader and deeper knowledge of...'.

Such objectives are too vague, too much like 'warm fuzzies', for training specialists like Robert Mager and Dugan Laird. In their approach to learning they emphasize the need for behavioural objectives which define participants' terminal behaviour and determine the progress of a course. Indeed in modern training there is an increased emphasis on employee performance and accountability for learning. Clear and measurable objectives for a training course are seen as necessary for both the trainer and the learner, and are used to explain and justify training to management. Contrary to Knowles' view however, training objectives need not lead to trainer-centred courses and a 'narrow learning path'. Well stated and relevant objectives can provide a clearly marked highway along which the trainer and participants can travel purposefully. Indeed, if you don't clearly know where you are going when you set off on a journey, you are highly likely to get lost.

Training applications

In recent years the importance of objectives, standards of performance and levels of competence within organizations has been highlighted by the development of competence-based training and assessment systems. In the UK the National Council for Vocational Qualifications (NCVQ) defines competence as: *The ability to perform in work roles or jobs to the standard required in employment*. The National Vocational Qualifications (NVQ) system is based on clearly defined national standards of competence developed and agreed upon by the organizations and people involved in a specific occupation. A competence-based system like NVQ:

- Involves the assessment of actual performance on the job.
- Is based on explicit standards and statements of performance defined by each industry. The standards are detailed and leave no room for doubt or misinterpretation.
- Is independent of any specified training programme. This makes it possible for people who have learned through experience on the job to be assessed and certified.
- Requires the collection of assessment evidence from the observation of workplace performance supplemented by other methods like questioning or testing.
- Is based on *criterion-referenced* assessment. This involves measuring people's performance against specific criteria or standards, rather than comparing them with each other. People either meet the standard and pass, or they fail and need additional training and retesting. In *criterion-referenced* assessment we expect the majority of people to meet the criteria and those who do not will be trained and assessed again. This compares with *norm-referenced* assessment generally found in traditional academic settings where people are compared to each other: candidates may be rated excellent, good, satisfactory or poor and only a fixed percentage might pass an examination.

The advantages of such a competence-based system are that it:

- Highlights the potential of the workplace as a learning resource and as a learning environment.
- Focuses on the assessment of outputs or outcomes of performance. Was the procedure completed correctly? Was the product quality to standard? Is this person competent in this task? Can he or she do the job?
- Provides clear guidance to assessors regarding the additional evidence to be collected. In particular, NVQ candidates need to show that they can apply their knowledge and skills to other situations, to transfer that competence

from place to place and context to context. They also need to demonstrate an ability to respond to changes in work practice, technology and methods.

■ Produces individualized assessment for job certification or further training.
■ Encourages safe working practices and the creation of a safe working environment.

The introduction of the NVQ system benefits industries and employers in the following ways:

■ NVQs provide information that can be used for recruitment, to guide the development of training programmes and to improve the cost-effectiveness of training.
■ A baseline for competent job performance and individual employee skill levels is established. Objective evidence is provided on whether individual employees can perform to set standards. In this way, the skills of the whole workforce can be audited and training needs can more clearly be identified.
■ Through their involvement supervisors can improve their training, assessment and performance review skills. Indeed, work on NVQs can provide supervisors and line management with objective evidence for the performance review process and direct their attention to performance rather than 'personalities'.

The introduction of the NVQ system also benefits *individuals* in a variety of ways:

■ Success is not dependent on examination ability. People who were unsuccessful at school and in formal examination situations have the opportunity for a 'fresh start'.
■ NVQs help people focus on what they do at work and to compare themselves with 'best practice' in their field. By providing clear goals, they can motivate people and encourage them to become more effective in their daily work.
■ NVQs can be built up and added to later. They provide a development pathway and are transferable to other organizations.

Competence-based training and assessment with its focus on clear measures of performance can stimulate and provide a clear structure for adult learning at the workplace. However, there are some criticisms made of the approach. These include:

■ A tendency to find competence because you are looking for it. Sometimes there may be a bias towards positive findings rather than an accurate assessment of job performance.
■ A focus on assessment-related issues at the expense of questions about how to train and educate people to make them more effective.
■ A dependence on supervisors as assessors. There is a great need for the development of effective observation tools and the structured training and development of assessors. The system stands or falls on the credibility of assessors and the assessment process.

More detailed information on workplace assessment can be found in Chapter 6, on how to evaluate training and job performance.

Certainly there are 'teething' problems in implementing competence-based training and assessment systems but the potential benefits are immense, particularly in manufacturing and service industries.

As we have seen, learning takes place more readily in some circumstances than in others. These ten factors which promote adult learning and the likelihood that training will be successful are linked: an effective training course and trainer will take account of most, if not all of them. In the following chapters we will see how these learning factors can be taken into account during needs assessment, course design, the development of course materials, course delivery and evaluation.

Project Action Items: Training in your organization

1. Think of something you learned recently. Write down a few words explaining why you were successful.

   _____

2. Think of something you tried to learn but were unsuccessful in learning. Write down a few words explaining what went wrong.

   _____

3. List at least three benefits that your organization can obtain from its investment in training.

   _____
   _____
   _____

4. Identify an area in your organization where training investment is needed and can be justified.

   _____
   _____

5. Describe a specific performance problem in your organization which can be helped by means of training.

   _____
   _____
   _____

2

How to identify staff training needs and involve the client

Before we start training people we need to identify as accurately as possible what their needs are. This chapter describes how to conduct an assessment of training needs and ensure the involvement of the client. It also shows how, through a needs assessment, you can gather resources and gain support for the development of a training programme.

When instructors discuss needs there tend to be differences of emphasis between those who are concerned with adult education and those who are involved in the training of adults. Adult educators generally view needs in terms of people's desires for self-improvement. Malcolm Knowles (1980) writes: 'An educational need is the discrepancy between what individuals (or organizations or society) want themselves to be and what they are; the distance between the *aspiration* and reality'. People involved in training however, are mainly concerned with increasing the effectiveness of individuals and their contribution to organizational productivity. They therefore think in terms of competence requirements or work performance, and see needs as essentially *performance discrepancies* or deficiencies. Dugan Laird (1985) writes: 'A training need exists when an employee lacks the knowledge or skill to perform an assigned task satisfactorily'. This chapter is primarily concerned with the assessment of training needs and will use as an example a needs assessment conducted for a new employee induction course.

Most people would agree about the value of induction courses and the need for induction whether someone is starting work in a college, hospital, a small business, or in a large-scale corporation. If asked to develop an induction course for new employees, you would probably have some good ideas about what was required – what information people would need to know; what new staff should be able to do within the induction period – if only from your own experience of joining the organization. But in order to produce an effective induction you would require information from other people in the organization. You would need to conduct some kind of needs assessment. Here are some of the major benefits of conducting such a needs assessment before developing training.

Benefits of conducting a needs assessment

A needs assessment has the following advantages. You can use it to:

Provide necessary information on participants

Before developing any kind of training, you need to find out as much as possible about your *target population*, the people you are going to train. You should know the number of prospective participants, their distribution (where they live and work), their age-range, the types of job they do, their interests, and any other important information. Robert Mager (1991) is a great advocate of target population studies and he says:

Not only will careful thought about your students help determine the starting point of the course, but it will help shape the course itself. It will help determine which examples are most likely to fit, what vocabulary to use, and even what instructional media and procedures to adopt.... If you spend even a tenth as much time thinking about and describing your students as you do thinking about your subject, you will develop a powerful tool for ensuring the effectiveness of your instruction.

At the end of a needs assessment for an induction course, you should be able to produce a brief description of the new employees – how many there will be, in which job areas they will be working, and their likely background. You should also have information on how employees might react to learning this information or set of skills, and their attitudes to the training methods which are likely to be used. For example, you will probably find that participants in an induction need more *getting to know you* activities and prefer presentations to be followed by discussions where questions and concerns can be easily raised.

Identify employee difficulties and performance problems

A needs assessment identifies the knowledge or skill needs of employees, and what the organization wants them to know or to be able to do. For example, an induction needs assessment should identify what the organization 'needs' new employees to know, what adjustments they have to make, the difficulties they face – particularly in the early weeks of employment. Some of these difficulties might be overcome through training, but others might require different forms of intervention eg, increased management involvement with new staff or adjustments in company procedures. Indeed your needs assessment should indicate to you what training can and cannot achieve.

Identify important topic areas

These areas might become modules in your training course. For example, modules in a company induction might deal with:

- The problem areas for new employees; adjustment and survival concerns.
- The company's mission, history and organization. This would show how the new employee's department contributes to the mission, fits into the organization, and how the employee fits in.
- Overview of departmental responsibilities and activities; what is expected of the new employee.
- Company personnel policy and benefits.
- Company performance review and merit system: how it will affect the new employee.

Provide documentation and materials for training

A needs assessment, particularly one which uses interviews or observation, gives you an opportunity to collect documentation from the field. For an induction course this might include manuals, organization charts, job descriptions, departmental procedures and forms, or samples of work. Such documentation might be included in an induction, handbook that can be used in the training session or for later reference. The critical incidents, anecdotes or examples that are obtained from interviews or observations might well be used as material for the development of case studies or role plays.

Provide information on attitudes to training.

If people do not believe they need to change then change is difficult. Even a cursory needs assessment will provide you with valuable information on people's feelings about the topic and the proposed training. In particular, it can identify and prepare you for problems that may arise during training. Through an induction needs assessment, you may find that supervisors do not attach much importance or spend much time on the induction of new staff. They may not be aware of the value of induction, the factors that impact negatively on a new employee, or how they can improve their own skill in giving induction to new employees. However, the very fact that a needs assessment is being conducted stresses to supervisors the importance of induction, and gives you an opportunity to provide suggestions that will help them conduct their own induction sessions more effectively.

Increase management and supervisory involvement

When you conduct a needs assessment it brings staff into contact with the prospective training at a formative stage. Managers and supervisors will be more interested in induction and more likely to contribute to the success of it, if they are consulted and their advice sought. If they are ignored with the implication that their help is not required, they may obstruct the training and ensure that it is unsuccessful. Similarly, participants will feel more involved and motivated if they see that you are trying to gear the training as closely as possible to their specific needs and to what they and their management want.

If you spend more time in your needs assessment on increasing involvement, this may have more impact in terms of successful results than if you spent that time on making minor improvements in the training.

Help establish contact with subject specialists

During a needs assessment, try to find out who might help with the development or implementation of training. When starting to develop a course, it is often useful to consult staff you interviewed or met during the needs assessment. Then, during the training session, subject specialists might come in and give brief presentations on their own particular field. For example, a representative of the personnel department and the company technical librarian are often useful guest presenters at a company induction. After the induction, those staff you identified during the needs assessment as being prepared to help new employees could act as *mentors* – experienced staff who provide informal assistance to new employees.

Help you estimate the cost of training

Before you can estimate the cost of training, you need to assess the training requirement. A needs assessment enables you to answer the following questions:

■ How important is the training? The relative importance of the target population and the number involved are critical here.
■ Who needs to be involved: trainers, department managers, specialists from other departments eg, personnel?
■ How long is it likely to take to develop the training?
■ When must the training be ready and when can it be conducted?

Using this information, you can estimate the cost of meeting the training requirement and report to management accordingly.

Save time, money and resources

Time and money are wasted if training is not targeted to needs. In some cases you may find that training is not the best solution or is only one of the solutions to a problem. An induction needs assessment may show that some problems may be solved by relatively simple and cheap methods, for example by producing checklists or other job aids to be used at the job site. The induction then might include introducing these job aids and giving new staff and/or their supervisors practice in using them. More information on job aids is given in Chapter 4.

Help you tailor the service acurately

Training is a service and provides a variety of products – training courses, training materials (checklists, videos etc.) and consultancy services. Just like any other service which produces a variety of products, training needs to constantly tailor the service and the products to fit changing customer requirements and interests. Your needs assessment therefore can serve as a market research tool, matching the service and the product to a particular customer's demands. For example, you would tailor an induction to the specific needs of new staff. It would however, be necessary periodically to adjust the induction to cater for changes in the company, changing jobs and changing staff needs.

Provide a means of measuring training effectiveness

A needs assessment should identify specific needs and potential objectives. In particular, it can generate data that will be useful in measuring the impact of training. If you do not conduct a good needs assessment, there is a tendency to try to cover everything in a course. This is the 'buckshot approach to training' where trainers aim to hit the needs of their target population by trying to cover everything. This *ready, fire, aim* approach often leads to the inclusion of a lot of irrelevant material in the course and promotes dissatisfaction and boredom among participants. For example, induction courses are sometimes filled with information that all the different departments think people should know. There may be little effort to tailor this information to the needs of new staff who are left to sort through what's presented to them and find out what is relevant.

If you do not conduct a needs assessment and your training does not adequately deal with participant needs, your programme is likely to be ineffective. Indeed you cannot evaluate the success of your training unless it's directed towards the accomplishment of actual learning needs. You can not judge how to improve the programme, whether the programme worked and whether the expense of time and money was justified. For example, did staff who had gone through the induction course feel better prepared? Did supervisors report fewer problems with new people? Was early attrition reduced? By identifying staff and organizational needs, a needs assessment provides the means of measuring the effectiveness of training and a way of demonstrating this to management (see Chapter 6 on evaluation of training).

For all these reasons a needs assessment can be an extremely valuable tool but there are some potential dangers to avoid. These include:

■ *Forgetting the KISS principle – Keep It Short and Simple*. Large-scale and expensive needs assessments can raise high expectations among customers and prospective participants, then lead to a big let-down. When too many people are involved in the project there may be confusion and unnecessary delay in taking action. By the time the assessment is completed, the problem may already have been solved or another more important one have come along. Indeed, in a time of rapid technological and organizational change, by the time you've set up a 'task force and taken six months to look at the situation', the problems and situations you were dealing with may no longer exist.

So a large-scale and expensive needs assessment may discredit a training programme before it is even developed. Critics may comment that more time and effort were put into the assessment than into the development of the training. The arguments of those who do not want trainers or anyone else involved in their business – the 'Trainers should stick to the classroom' brigade – are strengthened.

■ *Failure to identify the client's purpose.* Needs assessments can sometimes be used as a means of delaying action on a problem. The management or individuals requesting the assessment may hope that by the time there's a report, the pressure to do something about a problem will have diminished or disappeared. Alternatively, a needs assessment may be requested to justify, and give respectability to, what the client has already decided. Before starting a needs assessment, and at the first interview with the client, you must find out his or her attitudes and views. Has any kind of needs assessment been done before? Perhaps it was discarded as it didn't fit what managers wanted, or perhaps it has been forgotten! What, if anything, has already been decided? What is still open for decision? Have important people already made up their minds? Is this needs assessment meant to be a rubber stamp?

From the above it can be seen that even a relatively brief and simple needs assessment can greatly improve the quality of your training, increase its effectiveness and enhance the credibility of training with management and staff. This applies to all kinds of training settings whether in a college, company, or large organization.

Prepare for and respond to a training request

One of the most important distinctions in training is that between *proactive* and *reactive* trainers – those who are actively anticipating and looking for business, and those who are passively waiting for business to come to them. Among the main things that distinguish proactive from reactive trainers are their attitudes to needs assessments and the way they carry them out.

Proactive trainers realize that training is a service and, like any effective service group, are involved in conducting an ongoing needs assessment of their organization. They monitor company operations, personnel moves and policy or procedural changes. In response to developing organizational needs, proactive trainers prepare for and often prompt training requests.

Prepare for/prompt a request

Trainers keep in touch with the organization and its current and future training needs by:

■ Building up background files and resources from organizational literature, training magazines, books and other sources. Proactive trainers stay in touch with changes in the organization. They also keep up with current developments in training and education: subscribe to training magazines; build up a library of books and training resources; and are members of professional associations like the British Institute of Personnel Development (IPD) or the American Society for Training and Development (ASTD).

■ Maintaining close contact with other people and departments. Proactive trainers know what is about to happen before the event: when new staff are arriving; new projects being set up; new equipment being installed or new policies introduced. Rather than depend on formal communication, proactive trainers develop personal contacts or *networks* in other departments. They use training courses and discussions with participants to increase their knowledge of what is happening in the organization, what problems and opportunities might be developing, and how they relate to training. Proactive trainers are therefore constantly looking at how training can help staff respond to their own and organizational needs.

■ Forecasting future needs as the organization develops and changes. There is a tendency for needs assessments to focus on current problems and look back at the past problems that employees describe. Proactive trainers however look forward and attempt to forecast needs. They try to identify trends within their organization eg, changes in equipment, increased interest in *self-managed learning*, the introduction of total quality management (TQM). Proactive trainers stay ahead of the game and are therefore prepared when a training request comes.

Reactive trainers on the other hand respond to events and training requests, rather than actively shape them. They tend to wait for requests to come or for

Figure 2.1 *Prepare for and respond to training request*

instructions from 'above'. One result is they sometimes wait themselves out of a job. Reactive trainers generally do not carry out ongoing needs assessments (nobody told them to), and their contact with other departments and organizations is often formal and bureaucratic. Informal communication and *networking* may indeed be discouraged and treated as a threat. As a result when reactive trainers receive a training request, it comes unexpectedly, 'out of the blue', and they are unprepared.

As a proactive trainer, here are some of the steps you might take when you receive a request for training.

Respond to the request

No matter how your training requests arrive – by telephone, letter, as a result of a meeting, or through your own management's instructions – you should ensure that your own management is involved and knows what is going on. If a request is written, it's usually best to consult with your management and then respond in writing. If the request is verbal, respond verbally, and perhaps outline what might be contained in a formal written request to your management. You might set up an early meeting with the people making the request but make no commitments before you assess the situation.

Prepare for interview

When you're preparing to interview a prospective client you should ask yourself questions such as:

- *What information, materials do we have already?* Look through your resource materials, question colleagues who have dealings with the client department, collect information on your client's past and current involvement in training. Use your contacts to start building up a project file.
- *What lies behind this request?* Based on the information and materials gathered, try to assess what might lie behind this request for training. When meeting the client you will need to get beyond any vague generalized reasons for training. Find out what forces have moved him or her to make the request and the specific reasons for the request.
- *What do we want from this meeting?* Discuss the prospective meeting with colleagues if they are attending the meeting or may be involved in this project at some stage. Decide what your purposes are, what information you need, and what results you want from the meeting. Determine your role at the meeting; there are three common roles in this kind of situation – the trainer as a *subordinate*, as an *expert*, or as a *collaborator*. Here are some of the features of these roles:

   Trainer as subordinate. In this situation the client decides and tells you what the needs are and what solutions are required. This is the reactive trainer's role and as the client has already decided what training is required, there is often little or no needs assessment. If you develop a training programme to implement these decisions, prepare to fight with the client over responsibility for failure.

Trainer as expert. In this situation you decide and inform the client what the needs are and what solutions are required. This is a proactive trainer role but again one which tends to eliminate a preliminary needs assessment. If you develop a training programme to implement your own decisions without checking the client's needs, you will probably blame the client's organization, lack of support, or the unmotivated participants for any failure.

Trainer as collaborator. This role involves the trainer collaborating with the customer to arrive at a joint understanding of staff needs and the problems facing the organization. You then work together to conduct a needs assessment and implement a training programme based on the needs assessment. This joint collaborative approach prevents any adversarial relationship developing and any possible recriminations. The client becomes involved in and committed to the needs assessment, the development of training and ultimately, the success of the programme. Based on the foregoing, the role of collaborator is likely to be the most productive and is the one recommended here.

Interview client

The initial meeting with a client is preferably conducted at their work site. This shows that you're not a classroom or office-bound trainer and gives you some initial 'feel' for the client and their situation. This first meeting with the client should be fairly informal and essentially exploratory. You might however follow these steps.

Clarify the client's situation

At the beginning of the interview, establish and clarify your client's work

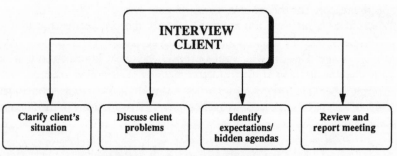

Figure 2.2 *Consult with/interview client*

situation. Find out about the organization, the client's position in the organization, the target population for training and what, if any, previous training has been given. Establish the political dimensions – who are the decision makers on this project, who else (eg, subject matter specialists, other departments) will be involved. Find out as much as possible about the relationships of people to each other, and make sure that no important group which should be involved in the training is left out. It is surprising how often people sometimes resist or even sabotage training projects out of a feeling that they have not been sufficiently consulted or informed at the beginning.

One of the most important things you need to find out is who will be the contact person, the *subject matter specialist*, in the client's department. You have to be careful here: the subject matter specialist may already have done quite a lot of work on the project with which you are becoming involved. He or she may feel touchy and defensive about the project, particularly with the involvement of 'outsiders'. Certainly do not, at this early stage, express criticism of what the subject matter specialist has done. You will probably need the specialist's assistance so it's useful to make him or her an ally at the beginning.

Discuss client problems

Through questioning you can help the client identify possible performance problems and what the specific needs of employees might be. You want the client to do most of the talking at this stage so exploratory questions are best. For example: What problems do you think there are? Would you say more about that? Could you be more specific? What would you like to see? Help the client discuss the situation mainly in terms of problems, opportunities, symptoms and causes – not in terms of what the solutions might be; that would be anticipating the results of the needs assessment.

It is particularly useful at this stage if you can refer to similar situations in other departments or elsewhere. Clients are always pleased to hear that other people have similar problems and that you have previous experience in this area.

Identify expectations and hidden agendas

At this meeting it is useful to identify the client's expectations – what results they expect or wants from the training. These expectations will influence the approach you take in the needs assessment and of course the formulation of training objectives. If the expectations seem unrealistic however, you should let the client know.

At this initial meeting you should also try to identify the client's *hidden agendas* – the hidden intentions, fears or concerns that lie beneath the surface and may have led to this request. There may be political sensitivities that the client is reluctant to speak about, a low-performing part of the department, some obstructive supervisors, attrition problems. It is best to find out these things at the beginning rather than in the middle of the needs assessment, or worst of all in the middle of the training.

Towards the end of the meeting your client will want to discuss possible time-scales or deadlines for the project. Some clients tend to believe that they are your only customer – that you have been sitting waiting for them to come along and now their problems merit your undivided attention. It is therefore best to limit your commitments at the initial interview. You will have to report to your own management and consider your own current workload.

Review and report meeting

Following the initial meeting with the client, it is important to review the situation and the information you have gathered. In particular you need to consider:

- What is the target population for possible training? How important are they to the company's operation? How numerous are they? What is the likely training time/cost per participant? Might some of the training you develop be used with other groups? These are important criteria for making decisions and your answers to these questions need to be reported.
- What is the likely support, interest level, or commitment of the client and key decision makers in the organization? What is their attitude towards the project, the possible training and to you, the trainer? Training does not take place in an ideal world and you need to identify the client's 'political' situation and the possible constraints and deal with them. This kind of *situation analysis* is critical at the beginning of a training project.
- Is training really the best way to deal with this situation? There may be other alternatives that you could recommend to the client: it may be possible for employees to be shown rather than trained; supervisors might give informal on-the-job training; job aids might be produced, or checklists used. Your role might be to help the client to implement these alternatives to training.
- Would training really solve, or help solve the problems? Rather than starting off with your training menu and finding needs to justify the use of that menu or the introduction of a new 'flavour of the month' course, you need to look at the actual needs within the organization. In many cases more than training is needed – changes in the customer's department and the systems used might well be more effective. In these cases organizational development interventions are likely to be more successful than training.
- Finally you should report to your own management. Depending on the cost and importance of the training, a written report may range from a memo to a written proposal with an action plan. This memo or proposal is usually best followed by a meeting with your management to discuss the project and any matters you may not have put in writing. If management approval is given for you to go ahead with the training, you might then set up a second meeting with the client.

Plan the needs assessment

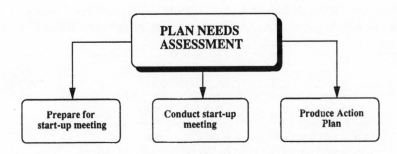

Figure 2.3 *Plan needs assessment*

Planning the needs assessment goes on prior to, during and after the 'start-up' meeting with the client.

Prepare for start-up meeting

Determine the specific purposes of this meeting – what additional information you require, what you want to achieve, the type of situation or project you want to be involved in. In short, you need to decide the next steps in your collaboration.

Conduct start-up meeting

This second meeting is more formal and structured than the first. At this second meeting you might do some of the following.

Discuss the results of your project review and the response from your own management. Find out if the client has received any input from his or her management on the initial meeting. At this stage 'new ideas' tend to arise and these should be discussed.

Ask your client and the subject matter specialist to separate their suggestions for training into *need to know* and *nice to know*. Here you are actually starting your needs assessment, with the client and subject matter specialist as your first respondents. Point out that *need to know* information and skills will certainly be covered and *nice to know* get covered if there is time. Subject matter specialists tend to think that everybody needs to know everything but a little gentle probing, requests for examples and questions about the target population's work situation should help you reduce the *need to know* information and skills to manageable proportions.

Collect or request additional resources such as job descriptions, operating manuals or policies and procedures. These will help you focus on operational needs and contribute to the credibility of your training. Again you should divide these resources into *need to know* and *nice to know*. The former can be dealt with in the training session. The *nice to know* materials may be used for reference and included in a participants' handbook.

Discuss responsibilities and agree on the client's and the specialist's involvement and responsibilities in the project. Try to get them involved from the

	ACTION STEPS	TIME FRAMES
1.	Training unit carries out a needs survey. A selection of department managers, supervisors and relatively new staff are interviewed individually to assess induction needs. Documentation and resources for the programme are collected	
2.	Training unit reports to management on the needs survey	
3.	Based on the needs survey, training unit develops: a) A job induction checklist for supervisors b) A workshop for supervisors on how to conduct job induction of new staff c) A company induction workshop for new staff	
4.	Training unit sends induction packages to department managers. Package includes: a) Copy of induction needs survey b) Outline of proposed induction programme c) Copy of job induction checklist for departmental review and input d) Nomination forms for supervisors' workshop and company induction workshop	
5.	Following input from departments, training unit revises job induction checklist and sends final printed copies to department managers and supervisors	
6.	Training unit conducts workshops for supervisors and trains them how to use the job induction checklist	
7.	Unit supervisors use job induction checklists with new staff	
8.	Training unit conducts company induction workshop	
9.	Training unit visits departments to follow-up and assist supervisors and new staff	
10.	Training unit reports to management on status and effectiveness of induction programme	

Figure 2.4 *Company induction action plan*

beginning and throughout the project to ensure their continuing commitment and involvement. This collaborative approach should prevent many problems arising.

Decide who will be required to participate in the needs assessment and make arrangements to meet them. The client and the subject matter specialist can help with the selection of staff, arrangements and procedures. For most needs assessments it is recommended that you meet the people one level up from the target population as well as the target population itself. A good sample is needed, however, and while collaborating with the subject matter specialist, try to ensure that you are not just put into contact with the 'company people'.

Decide the schedule for your needs assessment, particularly the reporting times and the time for completion of the assessment. Deadlines need to be realistic and allowance made for unforseen delays. A failure to meet mutually agreed deadlines at the first stage of a training project not only delays the whole training programme but, perhaps more critically, can undermine your credibility with the client and the target population.

Decide with your client how the results of the needs assessment will be recorded – if you use a questionnaire, you may need computer support. Decide also how these results will be communicated and to whom.

Produce an action plan

For an important and large-scale needs assessment it is advisable to develop an action plan. This formalizes the conduct of the needs assessment, the methods used, the timeframes, and when and how results will be communicated to management. As an example, Figure 2.4 shows an action plan for a company induction program.

Select and produce needs assessment tools

One needs assessment tool or technique will not fit all problems. You must select the appropriate technique or combination of techniques for the specific situation. A combination of needs assessment techniques may be preferable because if you study the appropriate staff and their jobs in at least two independent ways, you more than double your chances of being on target.

Your selection of the method or combination of methods to be used in a needs assessment mainly depends on:

■ The purposes of the assessment – whether you are identifying training needs at the organizational, job or task levels.
■ The size and operational importance of the target population. A large or operationally important group of people would justify the time and money spent on a detailed needs assessment.
■ The degree of resistance to training. A close involvement with the target

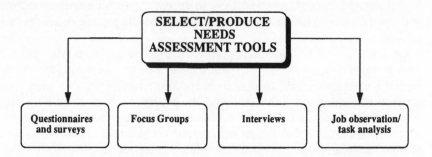

Figure 2.5 *Select/produce needs assessment tools*

population and their supervisors using methods like focus group discussion and interview is sometimes required in order to overcome resistance to 'controversial' training.

■ The type of data required. *Hard data* are the facts or information you can retrieve from reports on areas like production, defective parts, sales, absenteeism, or resignations. Such reports provide numbers that you can count, analyse and translate into statistics. Hard data can also be obtained through job observation and task analysis; these can identify how frequently a task is performed, how critical it is and what the specific steps in a task are. *Soft data* are the information obtained through such methods as group discussion, interviews and questionnaires. Soft data are subjective but can often be supported by hard data.

We will now look at the most commonly used needs assessment tools, moving from questionnaires – the least costly per response, to focus groups, interviews, job observation and task analysis – which tend to be more expensive.

Questionnaires

Benefits
The benefits of using a questionnaire are that it:

■ Can reach many people quickly. This is an important advantage when time is short and information has to be collected from a lot of people.
■ Is relatively inexpensive. Compared to focus group meetings, interviews and job observation, questionnaires are a relatively cheap way of gathering information.
■ Is easy to administer and, as it provides a familiar format for responses, *should* be easy for respondents to complete.
■ Gives respondents a chance to offer their own suggestions, ideas and opinions and express themselves without fear or embarrassment. Questionnaires should offer and safeguard anonymity.

■ Is completed in standard conditions. There are no face-to-face interview biases where the interviewer and interviewee may take a dislike to each other. Compared to the focus group meeting, interview, or job observation, the questionnaire is a 'cool' medium where emotional and unconsidered reactions are minimized.

■ Provides a lot of data that can be quantified, summarized and reported to management.

■ Can promote interest, involvement and support for a new project, a fresh approach or a new training programme.

■ Can impress the organization with the positive approach and responsiveness of the training unit to company needs.

Limitations

There are however some limits to the usefulness of questionnaires:

■ Questionnaires tend to be more effective at obtaining general information and opinions, rather than detailed information about job performance and training needs. Because many people resist providing detailed answers questionnaires are often not useful for gathering information on job performance.

■ Questionnaires only obtain answers to the questions that are asked. Contrary to appearances, it is not easy to write good questions and produce an effective questionnaire. Too often there are items that do not ask the right questions and questionnaires that are too long.

■ Low response rates can distort findings. Those who feel strongly, either for or against the proposed training, will tend to respond to the questionnaire.

■ Questionnaires generally fail to produce much accurate or precise job information. They are used most often when there is a low demand for accuracy or the trainers are already familiar with the situation and feel fairly confident of the training needs.

■ Questionnaires are often best constructed after several interviews have provided a framework and suggested some productive questions. It is often necessary to check and clarify responses to a questionnaire by conducting a few interviews. As mentioned previously, if the staff and their jobs are studied in at least two independent ways, we more than double our chances of being on target.

■ You should use questionnaires only if you are prepared to report the findings – the unfavourable as well as the favourable – and do something about these findings. Questionnaires reach many people in a formal way and they will want to know what you found out and what you are going to do about it.

A common trap that trainers fall into is using a questionnaire to ask managers to make an annual prediction of their training needs. Commenting on this Dugan Laird (1985) says,

Line managers don't know their training needs! So they either ignore the assessment, or send it in with misleading and superficial data....There's another problem growing out of asking managers to tell the Training and Development specialists their training needs: they come to believe that they do know how to determine training needs. Over a period of time they begin to demand training for performance problems which training won't solve.

General questionnaires on training needs can therefore put trainers in the difficult position of seeming to dissuade managers from carrying out training.

How to produce a questionnaire

■ Decide together with the other people involved in the training project (client, subject matter specialist, other trainers) what you want to know, why you want to know it and what could happen as a result of the assessment.

■ Include other trainers in your questionnaire design and gain the value of other perspectives and ideas.

■ Decide how you will analyse and report the data. Are you going to use a computer scoring system? What kind of reports will you need? Take account of these factors as you design the questionnaire and develop the questions.

■ Begin with a few non-threatening and easy to answer information items. Controversial questions at the beginning can cause defensive and dishonest responses. When they are faced with ambiguous questions – or questions they think may be dangerous to their position – people will often tell you what they think you want to hear.

■ Provide a mixture of *forced choice* and *open-ended* items. A *forced choice* item provides respondents with a series of options from which they must choose. A common type here is the question which asks respondents to rank problems, topics, or tasks in order of importance or frequency. For example, 'Read through this list of tasks and indicate how often you perform each task by circling *frequently, sometimes, infrequently*, or *never*'. By contrast, the open-ended item does not narrow the range of possible responses. For example, 'What problems do you encounter in conducting performance review meetings?'.

■ Make questions or items as brief as possible. Long, complicated questions make respondents lose interest – they may feel they do not have enough time to answer and will be critical of your questionnaire. In particular make use of Yes/No, data reporting items and those which require a specific response. For example, 'What practice activities do you think would improve the training programme?'.

■ Use simple and direct language. Avoid ambiguous, bureaucratic, technical or colloquial language. Bureaucratic language in particular indicates the 'establishment mind'; it will tend to irritate intelligent respondents – the ones who will give you really valuable information.

■ Avoid double-barrelled items. Do not ask respondents to answer more than one statement or question at a time. When in doubt, make one item into two.

- Do not use negatively worded items. These are easy to misinterpret. so you should reword the question or statement positively.
- Emphasize crucial words in each item by using bold lettering or underlining.
- Leave adequate space for respondents to answer open questions or to make their comments. These responses and comments may sometimes be difficult to categorize and quantify but they provide valuable data that your other questionnaire items may not be able to collect. It irritates the respondent if there is not enough space to answer a question, and it is frustrating for you to read small writing or responses that have been squeezed into the space.
- Group questions into coherent categories – do not force respondents to keep switching from one topic to another and then back again. This kind of content grouping makes it easier for you to analyse and compare responses.
- Test the questionnaire on representatives of, or a sample of the target population. Observe them as they complete it. What confusion, difficulties, ambiguities, did they encounter? How long did the questionnaire take to complete? How much flexibility was there and room for comment? Were there any problems with jargon or special terminology? Let the testers talk their way through the responses and discuss all the possible answers. Pilot testing in this way can often help you shorten and simplify the questionnaire.
- Make the questionnaire look professional. Print it and number the pages.

Focus groups

The main aim in using this needs assessment technique is to obtain information from a group of people familiar with the topic, the problem, or the product being discussed. A successful focus group activity can produce an honest assessment of training needs and involve the people with the needs in identifying and supporting training solutions. Usually a group consists of eight to twelve people together with one or preferably two facilitators. One facilitator might lead the discussion while the other records findings, asks for clarification or summarizes when necessary. Through the group discussion you can carry out an on-the-spot needs assessment and perhaps gain a measure of consensus. Group discussion can be expensive in terms of meeting time but it takes less time than a series of individual interviews and enables you to include more respondents in your assessment.

Benefits
Additional benefits of group discussion are that it:

- Provides valuable information when members represent a variety of viewpoints on a particular issue. The group discussion can often elicit information that individuals might not bring up on their own.
- Encourages a synthesis of different viewpoints. Through discussion, the organizational climate can be improved and conflict among course participants

can be reduced. In particular, the focus group can be used to defuse hostilities and negative attitudes to training. Indeed, if these can not be defused at a group meeting, you should discuss the situation with your client as it is likely that any subsequent training may be ineffective.

■ Can provide a measure of the importance or frequency of issues or tasks. The discussion and discussion findings will indicate how important or frequent something is so that you can adjust your training objectives accordingly.

■ Encourages a feeling of 'ownership' among participants. They are more likely to support training which is based on their own discussions, findings and recommendations.

■ Provides good training for supervisors in analysing problems. A group meeting can lead to a positive focus on how training can improve performance and solve problems, rather than a negative focus on how hard things are or who is to blame.

■ Can generate authentic case study, role-play and critical incident materials for use in training sessions.

Limitations

There may however be difficulties in using group discussion:

■ It is sometimes difficult to get the right people released at the same time.

■ Perhaps as a result of release problems, the group membership may be unrepresentative.

■ Information given at the meeting and the attitudes shown may be distorted by a recent event eg, redundancies, an accident, reorganization, or changes in management.

■ The public nature of the focus group meeting sometimes stifles honest discussion of actual job performance, feelings and causes.

■ The facilitator needs to establish a climate of trust and openness and this is difficult if participants see him or her as being close to management. In the same way a facilitator who is close to the topic – eg, the future role of the training unit – may be regarded as too involved. The objectivity of the focus group results may be questioned, especially if the facilitator writes the report.

■ A very skilled group facilitator is needed to encourage everyone to contribute, to focus the meeting and to handle any conflict or disruption. However, if the facilitator has an assistant to record findings and help guide the discussion, this makes the job more manageable and tends to improve the accuracy and acceptability of the results. (see the section on co-training in Chapter 5).

Interviews

If you really want to know how people feel about their work, the organization, the problems they face, and the areas where they think they need more training, you should ask them. Malcolm Knowles (1980) writes:

Interviews of some kind are a must for training officers.... Better than any other device, they help them to understand how people feel and why – understanding crucial to any effort to bring about change. They also demonstrate, in a personalized way, sincere interest in what people in the organization think.... Open-ended, non-directive interviews are more valuable than other kinds for getting at feelings and attitudes and at the causes of problems.

Interviews can be used as the main needs assessment technique or as a supporting technique. The rule of thumb is to use interviews as the main technique with small, high-status, target populations; where there are important sensitivities to consider; where the participants need to 'buy into' the training; and when the expenditure can be justified to management. As a supporting technique, you can use interviews to supplement data from questionnaires and job observations, and to verify or give a fresh perspective to those data.

Benefits
The benefits of conducting needs assessment interviews are that:

- People feel they are being consulted and listened to. Interviews help you build up rapport with individuals in the organization and to become familiar with their terminology and situation.
- If you and the interviewee can establish a good relationship, a lot of information can be shared in confidence within a short time.
- Interviews provide maximum opportunity for staff to freely express their opinions and give suggestions. Interviews encourage people to get things off their chests. Dugan Laird (1985) comments:

  When the issue of training is especially sensitive, or if strong feelings exist about certain programs... no assessment can measure the depth of the feelings; only interviews can permit that two-way, affective exchange.

- When people are interviewed they feel more interested and committed to the success of the needs assessment and the training. Interviews therefore are helpful in obtaining support for new training programmes.
- Interviews can serve as clarifiers – they give an opportunity for you to clear up assumptions, confusion, and ambiguities on the spot. They provide you with a clearer perspective and better understanding of the situation
- Interviews enable you to formally compare and contrast the experience, views and expressed attitudes of interviewees. For this reason it is helpful to use a structured interview guide (see Figure 2.6) so that you ask the same questions, cover the same topics and can make comparisons in the needs assessment report.
- Interviews are flexible. You can spend more time with productive respondents and adjust your interview style and question types to fit the personality of the interviewee. Laird (1985) comments:

  One big advantage of the interview is its flexibility. When pre-planned questions fail

Interview conducted by: _____

Place and date of interview: _____

Name(s) of interviewee(s): _____

Introduction and explanation of: background and purpose of interview, how the interviewee can help, structure and documenting of interview, reporting and confidentiality.

What problems do you think employees experience in this area?

_____

_____

_____

Critical incidents referred to/striking comments made by interviewee:

_____

_____

_____

What do you think employees should know about this topic?

_____

_____

_____

What do you think employees should be able to do in this area?

_____

_____

_____

(Interviewer gives an outline and some details of the proposed training.)
What are your views/suggestions on this proposed training?

_____

_____

_____

_____

What should I have asked you about, and haven't?

_____

_____

Resources eg, procedures manuals, performance review forms, data, etc. obtained from the interviewee:

_____

_____

(Interviewer explains what will happen to the information received and expresses appreciation for information and help given.)

Interviewee's contact telephone number: _____

Additional comments/observations: _____

_____

Interviewer's signature: _____ Date: _____

Figure 2.6 *Structured interview*

to hit pay dirt, or when unexpected 'agendas' of interviewees begin to appear, the interviewer can always move into an 'open and reflective question' mode to accommodate and encourage the unanticipated data.

■ Interviews are an intervention into an existing system or organization and can reinforce existing movements and pressure for change.

Limitations

There are however limitations and difficulties in using interviews for a needs assessment:

■ Interviews are expensive and time-consuming. You not only have to allow time for preparation and the actual interview, but for waiting time and, possibly, travel to the job site.
■ Successful interviews require good interviewing skills. If the interview is not handled well, an interviewee can become defensive, hostile and a potential opponent of the proposed training.
■ The interviewees may doubt that the interview will be held in confidence and may not answer questions candidly or fully. You may well encounter prepared model responses and deliberate cover-ups. You need to be able to spot these and handle them diplomatically, but also get beyond them.
■ There may be constant interruptions if the interviewee is poorly organized or has not asked someone to take the phone calls and deal with visitors.
■ There is always the danger of an 'us' and 'them' situation developing, and of you being identified or emotionally identifying yourself with the management, supervisors, or staff. In needs assessment interviews you should hold and be seen to hold a detached position.

Job observation and task analysis

Job observation and task analysis are used most often when the target population is large, the training programme expensive, and consequently there is a great need for accuracy. Remember Dugan Laird's statement: 'A training need exists when an employee lacks the knowledge or skill to perform an assigned task satisfactorily'. Here is a formula to help determine training needs:

$$C - I = D.$$

In this formula C = competence or what an employee must be able to do, I = inventory or what an employee can already do and D is a potential training need or deficiency.

Through job observation and task analysis we can see what the employee must be able to do, how he or she actually does it, and therefore identify the training need or deficiency.

Benefits

Job observation and task analysis have the following benefits as needs assessment techniques; they:

- Bring you into direct contact with the people you will be training, their jobs and their supervisors.
- Supplement or validate information gained from interviews and questionnaires.
- Provide hard data on the *actual* responsibilities and tasks involved in doing a particular job. For training and assessment purposes these tasks can then be broken down into a series of steps.
- Help you decide whether formal training is really necessary and whether alternatives – coaching, the use of job aids like task lists or checklists – may be more appropriate and cost-effective.
- Generate resource material for the training – examples from the job, case studies or simulations.
- Enable you to assess the work environment to determine what barriers may stand in the way of learning, skill transfer and the application of training. Job observation also enables you to judge factors in the environment that might be used to support the training.

Limitations

There are however a number of difficulties in using job observation and task analysis:

- Observation and analysis tend to be time-consuming and therefore expensive.
- Many jobs involve cyclical operations that take place on a weekly, monthly or yearly basis. A great deal of time would be necessary to observe and analyse these tasks. In this situation you might sit with the subject specialist(s) and talk through an operation. You need to be careful though: if a person is very experienced and does a job well, he or she may forget or ignore small but critical steps.
- The responsibilities and tasks that make up a particular job may differ from one employee to another and from one department to another. For example, the responsibilities and job tasks of a clerk in one department may differ from those in another department. You may need to identify *core tasks* – those which every person with that job title needs to be able to do and *optional tasks* – those which are peculiar to a specific department or unit. Flexibility therefore needs to be built into your analysis.
- The staff conducting the job observation or analysis may be treated as 'management spies' or 'time and motion' inspectors. The supervisors of the employees being observed may react with hostility to what they see as outside interference and the employees may see observation as a threat to their jobs. A hostile reaction can build up to any proposed training.
- There may be conflict among the subject specialists as different approaches

may be taken to the same task. One inspector may start with the documentation and then move to inspecting the equipment; another may start with the equipment before moving to the documentation. In any training you develop you will need to be flexible and unless a certain order of operations is necessary, place no restrictions on sequence.

■ Job observation is difficult for people not trained in the use of observation tools and task analysis. It also requires the observer to be self-effacing, a good listener and patient. If you intend to use job observation and task analysis as needs assessment tools, you will have to develop those skills and qualities.

■ There may be a conflict between the written instructions, what people should do and what people actually do. In this case you need to resolve the conflict with the client or subject specialists before you develop any training.

Indeed, before you start to develop a training programme based on job observations and/or task analysis you need to ensure consensus: the client and the subject specialists need to 'sign off' on the results of your observations or analysis.

Conduct the needs assessment

A needs assessment is an *intervention* into an existing situation; never expect to conduct an assessment in an atmosphere free of politics and difficulties. Expect some distrust, some resistance but also expect some changes in the situation. The Heisenberg Principle in physics states that the act of measuring the temperature of water with a thermometer changes the temperature. In the same way, the act of studying organizations and people changes the people and organizations being studied. Indeed the very fact that a needs assessment and job research are being conducted often encourages change. The sudden appearance of new approaches and solutions to problems may well coincide with your needs assessment.

Once you have chosen and produced the tools for the needs assessment you need to use them effectively. Here are some suggestions about how to use the different needs assessment tools we've discussed.

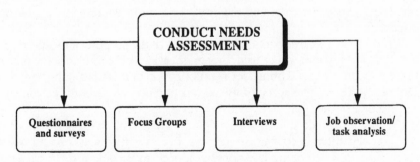

Figure 2.7 *Conduct needs assessment*

How to use a questionnaire

Attach a covering letter to your questionnaire. Give the reason(s) why respondents were selected and explain to them the purposes and importance of collecting this information. Explain how it may be used to benefit the organization and include a statement reinforcing the confidentiality of responses.

Provide clear concise instructions on how to complete the questionnaire. Give a reasonable deadline for completion, make sure there are clear instructions on what to do with the completed form, and include a self-addressed envelope.

Express appreciation for the time and effort respondents put into answering the questionnaire.

If the questionnaire is not completed on time, follow up with a tactful phone call. This will increase the return rate and therefore reduce any distortion caused by an unrepresentative sample.

Analyse the responses to the questionnaire. If you have grouped questions about the same content together, then trends and disagreements will be shown more clearly. It will also make it easier for you to produce a report.

How to use a focus group

In your preparation for the focus group meeting you need to take the following course of action.

Define the task or problem. For example, 'What are the induction needs of new staff and how can they be helped to adjust and become productive more quickly?'

Establish the objectives of the meeting. What will be the products of this discussion – a report, an action plan, a list of training recommendations?

Select a neutral location for conducting the discussion. A prestigious location will indicate the importance management attaches to this topic.

Select the participants. The group should ideally be composed of a representative cross-section of individuals who are, or will be, involved with the training. Limit the numbers. If there are more than 12 participants, the atmosphere becomes more public, there is a reduction in individual participation and an increase in the 'holding' back of information and opinions. Whatever you do, do not allow managers to 'observe' the group session. It will certainly inhibit open discussion.

Write a letter to participants informing them of the purpose of the meeting, its duration and where it will be held. You might also ask them to do some preparation for the meeting and bring specific information or materials along with them. Do not, however, give participants too much information about the content of the meeting or they may arrive with prepared statements.

Produce an agenda and a discussion guide. This may be a list of questions you will ask with three or four main questions to focus the discussion and perhaps some subordinate probing questions. You need to provide a structure for the discussion but at the same time stay flexible.

Here are some steps you might follow when you conduct a focus group meeting:

- Keep participants close to each other – the room should not be large and the arrangement of tables and chairs should encourage an intimate atmosphere. Make sure that tea and coffee are available and allow time for informal chatter at the beginning to establish relationships and a non-threatening atmosphere.
- Explain the purpose of the needs assessment, the objectives of the meeting and the specific information you are looking for. Emphasize the confidentiality of comments, that information will be treated as group data and no individual will be identified personally. Tell participants what you will be doing with the information you collect.
- Ask group members to introduce themselves, say what they do and how long they have been with the organization. They should give some information about their background and perhaps answer a question related to the topic. (For more information on suitable introductory activities see Chapter 5.)
- State the topic which gave rise to this meeting and the significance of the issue or questions on which you want information. You might then give participants a key question for them to think about.
- Give participants time to think and generate ideas and ask them to write things down in response to the question. This act of writing forces participants to think carefully about the question you raised and clarify their points.
- Finally, elicit participants' points one by one, with you or the recorder listing them on the flipchart. You should clarify anything which is unclear but avoid any discussion of points at this stage. Probe and follow-up questions can be used to clarify information. You should also clarify, or better still get the participants to clarify, any technical terms, jargon, or complex ideas which some of the group members may not understand.
- You might then conduct a small group activity where participants rank problems or issues in terms of importance. This forces your participants to consider seriously the relative importance of needs, problems and information. This type of ranking activity also encourages lively and purposeful group discussion.
- Groups should then report on the results of their ranking activity.
- Following the group reports you might have a general discussion. At the beginning you should use questions and statements that directly elicit contributions and encourage people to express their ideas and opinions. Then, as the discussion moves along, you can ask more specific questions that elicit additional details; for example, 'John, you mentioned that there is a training problem. Could you be more specific about that?'.

If a participant makes a strong statement or has an unusual idea, check with the others, but protect the original speaker from any hostility. Your role is to act as a facilitator – do not be threatening, encourage all contributions and be supportive, particularly in the critical first few minutes of the discussion. Later you can let participants carry the discussion and just keep them basically on track. Do not rush to fill pauses in the discussion though – a reluctant speaker might be gathering courage and about to join in, and other participants may be thinking.

■ The discussion should be followed by a summary. To ensure that nothing important has been forgotten, use a question like, 'We seem to have covered a lot of ground. Is there anything I should have asked or we should have discussed but didn't?'. You might then review with participants what has been written on the flipchart during the meeting and make any necessary adjustments. The chart thus provides you with a record of the meeting and one that has been endorsed by the group.

After the focus group meeting, your findings can be condensed into a short report for management. This report might identify the topics covered by the group, the main points that arose and the results or recommendations of the meeting. These recommendations might be in the form of a list of job responsibilities and tasks, training needs, or an action plan that participants produced. Following the meeting, the report can be sent to participants for their information and action.

How to use interviews

The attitudes of the interviewer and the interviewee are the keys to the development of an interview. In what might be called *hot interviews* respondents are eager to express their ideas and feelings and are likely to give you a lot of information. In *cool interviews* the respondent may be reluctant to contribute and you will need to draw out specific information from vague, generalized and evasive responses.

As an interviewer you also need to be aware of the concept of *noise* and its effect in interview situations. *Noise* is defined as 'what interferes with the smooth flow of information'. External noise consists of distractions like telephone calls or people coming in. Internal noise is the emotional disturbance inside the interviewee arising from differences in accent or nationality between you and him or her, defensiveness, aggressiveness, or insecurity. As a result of noise, respondents may not hear what you actually say but what they think you are saying. In order to conduct a successful interview therefore, you need to reduce both external and internal noise.

As mentioned previously, interviews are expensive. The number of interviews you conduct is largely dependent on the size and importance of the proposed training programme. It also depends on responses. When the stories begin to repeat themselves and you hear the same things from a variety of respondents (and this may happen earlier than you think) *stop*: you have completed this part of the needs assessment.

How to prepare for an interview

Arrange to conduct interviews with a cross-section of the target population and their supervisors.

Find out as much as you can about the interviewees' situation and, if possible, get to know something of the terminology used in this job area.

Arrange the meeting at the interviewee's convenience but avoid unnecessary delay or procrastination. Agree on a specific date and time.

Do not arrange for the meeting to be late in the day or just before lunch when thoughts turn to eating or going home. In particular, avoid meetings over lunch where the interviewee can evade the real issues.

Control, if possible, who will attend the meeting. An insecure or reluctant interviewee will sometimes invite other people to join in the interview session. This can sometimes be helpful and the information that others bring may be useful. However, do not let the interviewee escape the issues in this way.

Prepare and discuss your interview outline with a colleague. Test out the effectiveness of your questions to ensure that they fit your needs and situation (see Figure 2.6 as an example).

It is better to have too many questions than too few as sometimes you may be faced with a reluctant or taciturn interviewee. Be prepared to follow up on your general questions with specific ones.

Arrive a little early to be mentally ready for the interview and so that an hostile respondent can not complain about lateness.

How to conduct an interview

This section considers some general interview techniques and relates these to the sample induction needs interview, shown in Figure 2.8. When conducting an interview you need to consider the following points.

Establish the interview climate. Introduce yourself and try to put the interviewee at ease by being relaxed and friendly. Give something of the background to this needs assessment – who authorized it and its specific purposes. Explain that you are here because the interviewee is an expert in this area and you are seeking valuable advice and suggestions. Explain that you will take notes on the interview and reassure the interviewee about confidentiality.

The use of a form such as Figure 2.6 helps to structure the interview but can intimidate some people. Therefore it is sometimes best just to make notes on a blank sheet and transfer them to the form after the interview. During the interview you can also use note-making as a tool to clarify or slow the pace of responses with comments like, 'Could you explain that again?' or 'That's an important point. Let me make a note of it'.

A common interview approach is to sequence your questions from general to specific. General questions are used to broach the topic and give the interviewee a chance to expand. Then specific questions pin down facts and examples. For example, the induction needs interview in Figure 2.8 begins with a question about the problems faced by new staff. This is then followed by specific questions about the problems the interviewee mentions. If the interviewee begins to ramble, or confuse the discussion with jargon or vague generalities, you can use focusing questions or statements like 'I'm not sure I followed you then', or 'Could you give me an example?'

During an interview try to elicit, and make a special note of, any critical incidents mentioned, or striking comments made by the interviewee. Often a particular incident or comment illuminates a situation much more clearly than any series of interviews or reports. For example in the induction needs interview, it was mentioned that when the new employee worked in an area close to the manager's office, he or she was likely to receive a reasonable induction. This indicated that greater management interest would improve the inductions given by supervisors. Comments or critical incidents can also often be used in the development of case studies for a training programme.

Two critical questions in any training needs assessment are:' What should employees know?' and 'What should employees be able to do?'. In the induction needs assessment the *need to know* list is longer than the *need to do* list. This is typical of an induction situation where you have recruited someone qualified and experienced to do the job. His or her deficiencies are mainly knowledge deficiencies: they need to know *how* your particular organization does the job.

Throughout the interview, demonstrate concern and interest in what the interviewee is saying. You can make encouraging remarks like, 'I see', 'That's helpful', or repeat key words to stimulate further responses or as a query. Facial expressions, nodding of the head and encouraging noises like 'uh-uh' also reinforce the interviewee and encourage him or her to keep on talking. In order to summarize answers, double-check, or encourage further elaboration, use statements and questions like 'So what you're saying is...', 'Does this mean that...?'.

Don't let your form or list of questions become a straitjacket, and feel free to stray when the information is valuable and flowing freely. For example, interviewees may elaborate immediately on some points that you'd planned to ask about later or start to tell you about some significant incidents or examples.

Towards the end of an interview you might give an outline and some details of the proposed training. This is an opportunity for you to put the interviewee 'in the picture' and make him or her feel part of an *exchange* of information and ideas. You might ask for the interviewee's opinions on the proposed training. Here you are not only looking for information and suggestions, but assessing the interviewee's attitude to the training. This can be an opportunity to gain assistance and support; in the sample induction needs interview the response to mentoring and the suggested training for supervisors were indicators of strong support for training. If the interviewee's attitude is uninterested or hostile to training however, do not get into a personal argument. Listen to what the interviewee has to say, present the case as you see it and make sure you part on reasonable terms. People are more likely to change their minds *after* an interview than during it.

Conclude the main part of the interview with an open-ended question. For example, 'You've given me a lot of valuable information and ideas about the situation. What haven't I asked about that I should have?', or 'What aspect might we be overlooking?' This should encourage an interviewee to express his or her concerns about any controversial or sensitive issues.

An interview is an opportunity not just to collect information and ideas, but to gather resources as well. These might include procedures manuals, performance review forms, or other data the interviewee possesses. Collecting this kind of material from interviewees also involves them more closely with the training.

At the end of the interview, summarize some of the things you've learned. Tell the interviewee what you intend to do with the information and what action might be taken. Thank the interviewee for his or her time and the valuable input that will help you develop any training. If the interviewee seems to want to prolong the meeting, this may be because of a desire to discuss something sensitive so do not be in too much of a hurry to be off.

A section on your interview form for additional comments or observations will give you extra flexibility. You might write in additional points or ideas here during the interview, or after you have had time to consider.

Following a series of interviews your needs assessment report would summarize the most important information and opinions you obtained. In order to encourage further cooperation you might also send interviewees thank-you notes that emphasize how valuable their input has been to the needs assessment and the development of training.

How to use job observation and task analysis

No matter how much time you spend questioning clients and subject specialists about a particular job and its performance requirements, there is no substitute for actual observation. Indeed, if you do not observe before starting to conduct training, you may find out that the reality of the job differs a great deal from the description given by subject specialists, job descriptions, or other documentation.

As with interviewing, the Hiesenberg Principle operates when conducting job observation. The act of observing behaviour is likely to change that behaviour, especially when the observer's presence is very noticeable and regarded as threatening. Yet you need to see people working as usual and observe normal job behaviour to understand the factors that may be affecting performance.

When you use job observation as a needs assessment tool you may be concerned with refresher training or improving an already existing training programme. You may use a few observations in conjunction with interviews or other needs assessment techniques as a further *reality check*.

Task analysis is a more expensive and time-consuming process as it involves a detailed examination of each job task. The purpose generally is to develop a new and extensive job training programme. A task analysis can identify:

■ The tasks and task steps that are critical for successful job performance and therefore need to be included in training.

Interview conducted by: AMS

Place and date of interview: Computer Operations Dept. 18 Dec, 1994

Name(s) of interviewee(s): Tony Evans and Dave O'Connor

Introductions and explanation of: background and purpose of interview, how the interviewee can help, structure and documenting of interview, reporting and confidentiality.

What problems do you think new employees experience in this area?
Problems of employee adjustment in first few weeks. Supervisors don't have the time or skills to provide an effective induction programme. New employees have to learn a lot about the organisation, systems and procedures but are usually left to learn about it piecemeal. Each new employee is usually assigned to an experienced employee, but there is a problem of time.

Critical incidents referred to/striking comments made by interviewee:
Amount of help new employee gets from the supervisor tends to depend on how close he or she is to the manager's office. We have a fairly high attrition rate and a better induction programme might help. Supervisors don't expect 'high fliers' to stay long – there are too many other good opportunities; becomes something of a self-fulfilling prophecy.

What do you think employees should know?
How the department is organized – channels of communication.
How the deparment fits in with and serves other departments.
Department systems and procedures – identity cards, absence notification, holidays, correspondence and filing system, secretarial assistance.
Shift cycles – how they affect the new employee.
Company performance review system – merit increase, etc.
Safety information – evacuation plan and procedures.

What do you think employees should be able to do?
Basically learn and adjust to our way of doing things within the first month or so. Specifically new employees need to be brought 'up to speed' on the systems and equipment we're using.

Interviewer gives an outline and some details of the proposed training.

What are your views/suggestions on this proposed training?
Three-stage induction programme – department induction, unit induction and mentoring by experienced employees – sounds a good idea. Like the idea of mentoring (some units are already doing this) and some training for mentors. Would like supervisors to receive some training in how to provide a good induction programme. Job induction checklist for supervisors would be useful. The department is prepared to provide time to make induction effective.

What should I have asked you about and haven't?
Supervisors have become used to a high attrition rate and don't take induction very seriously. Attitude tends to be, 'if people stay, they stay. If they leave, they leave!'. Belief among some supervisors that 'sink or swim' approach is best. Supervisors don't want to take responsibility in this area. If they were given some ideas, guidance, a checklist like the one suggested, it would help.

Resources eg, procedures manuals, performance review forms, data, etc. obtained from the interviewee:

1. Department organisation chart.
2. Department information booklet that's given to new employees. Booklet needs updating before it can be used for induction purposes. Interviewees will see that it's updated. Units have their own specific documentation.
3. Names of a few supervisors and new employees who might usefully be interviewed.

Interviewer explains what will happen to the information received and expresses appreciation for information and help given.

Interviewee's contact telephone number: 573-8123

Additional comments/oberservations: It would be worthwhile interviewing several supervisors and new employees. These interviews would provide information for the department induction programme, updating of the department information booklet, development of the supervisor's job induction checklist, and for a training session for supervisors and mentors.

Interviewer's signature: **Date:**

Figure 2.8 *Induction needs interview*

■ The knowledge, skills and other characteristics required to adequately perform the necessary tasks.

■ The tasks or task steps that can be simplified or eliminated in order to prevent unnecessary training. When you develop a training programme you need to avoid training people in unnecessary tasks, procedures or process steps. One way to do this is to work with the client and subject specialists to flow-chart a particular process or review the steps in a task. Can any stages or steps be eliminated? Does this process or task continue because of tradition rather than current needs? How can the job be streamlined?

This information forms the basis for programme development and course content. Here are some suggestions about how you might conduct a task analysis.

How to conduct a task analysis

Develop an initial task list. Talk with the client and subject specialists and study existing documentation to get a general picture of the situation. If a previous job analysis has been conducted you might start the process there and then proceed to other sources such as job descriptions, procedure manuals and training materials. Supplement this material with other information gathered from observation, individual and group interviews with jobholders and supervisors, and interviews with management staff. Review all this information and prepare a preliminary task list for each job.

Meet with a panel of subject matter specialists to review and revise the initial task list. The first task analysis matrix in Figure 2.9 is a result of this kind of analysis and review. Each task is identified as being *core*, performed by everyone

Task Analysis: Administrative clerk

1. Initial task analysis

TASK NO.	CORE	LEVEL 1	LEVEL 2	LEVEL 3	REMARKS
1.01	YES	YES	YES	YES	Prerequisite for recruitment
1.02	NO	NO	YES	YES	Task is specific to one dept.
1.03	YES	NO	YES	YES	Training required
1.04	NO	NO	NO	YES	Task usually done by supervisor

Task No. – refers to the list of tasks
Core – indicates this task is done by everyone in the job
Level 1 – job entry level task
Level 2 – task can normally be completed to standard within one year
Level 3 – task can normally be completed to standard within three years or is a supervisory-level task

2. Core task analysis

CORE TASK	FREQ.	IMP.	LEARN DIFF.	REMARKS
1.01: Generates letters, memos, and handles correspondence	5	5	3	Spends up to 50% of the day
1.03 Produces statistical reports	5	5	4	Has taken PC courses
1.07 Inputs data into management information system	3	5	2	On a daily basis for about an hour
1.09 Orders stationery, storehouse and other materials as needed	2	2	2	On a weekly basis

Core task – indicates task done by everyone in this job.
Frequency, importance and learning difficulty are rated on a five-point scale with five marking a high degree of frequency, importance, or difficulty.

Figure 2.9 *Task analysis – administrative clerk*

in the job, or as not core, performed by only some job-holders. The level at which the task is performed is also indicated and the panel have made some remarks relevant to training.

In order to alleviate any fears about 'spying', explain the purpose and process of the observation to everyone involved. In particular, you might assure employees that this observation and any task analysis is for training purposes and that nothing seen or heard will be put in their personnel file. You might also explain that this is one of several observations at different job sites to familiarize you with the operation

Conduct your observation in two stages. The first observation would be to get a general idea of the job and its context. Any notes might be made on a blank sheet of paper. The second observation should focus on those aspects of the job that are important for the needs assessment. You might use an observation guide at this stage to focus your attention and allow for more structured note-making.

An observation guide might describe job actions or activities with narrative statements or a checklist format. It needs to be closely linked to the purposes of the needs assessment and should be simple to understand and use. Any guide should assess the relevant factors in the activity and accommodate qualitative and quantitative aspects of the job. For example the guide might include the frequency or percentage of the day spent in doing the task or using the skill, and the relative importance of the task or skill in the employee's job.

Verify and collect additional data from employees on the tasks they perform and the knowledge/skills involved. Check on the frequency with which a task is performed and how critical the task is as measured by the impact of inadequate performance. Information on criticality is essential to determine whether formal instructional time needs to be devoted to the task.

Restrict your activity to observing. In cases where individual coaching or training would improve performance or raise it to standard, make a note and discuss this with the supervisor. You might occasionally ask questions to clarify or gain additional details but try to focus on observation.

The second task analysis matrix shown in Figure 2.9 is a result of these observations and analyses the core tasks performed by an administrative clerk. The headings here are core task, frequency, importance (in terms of the requirements of the position), learning difficulty, and remarks. The tasks are specific rather than generic. The clerk 'Produces statistical reports' rather than the general 'Uses a PC'. Frequency, importance and learning difficulty are rated on a five point scale with five marking a high degree of frequency, importance or difficulty. The learning difficulty category indicates that this job observation is for training purposes. A remarks column on the form also provides useful flexibility and can be used to increase the focus on the purpose of the analysis.

Through job observation it is possible to identify the critical tasks, knowledge and skills necessary in order to perform a job. In particular, you can pinpoint those critical behaviours and performance factors that separate high- and low- performing individuals in a job. This *critical difference* information can provide a basis for making decisions on the selection and training of new employees and for choosing the content for refresher or advanced training programmes. For example, during a job observation you might discover that the quality of coaching and delegation of tasks make a critical difference in the supervisor's job and distinguish 'successful' supervisors from those who are less 'successful'. A training programme for supervisors therefore may well focus on improving coaching and delegation skills.

When job observation is for training purposes you might identify some of the potential barriers to successful training. These include the barriers the learner brings to the situation, those that the learner's direct boss creates, and the barriers that the organization contains. These potential barriers need to be reported to the client and taken into account in the development of the training course.

It is also important to find out from employees how *they* think job performance could be improved. Training and development courses are often more successful when they focus on what prospective participants see as most likely to improve current performance.

When the job observation is completed, write up your notes and consider your data. Did you miss out any important details? Is it necessary to check any further through additional observation, interviews, or discussion? In particular, check the reliability of your data. Agreement among observers is the basis for determining the validity of data and two or more observers of the same activity should have identical or at least similar descriptions.

Following the job observation or task analysis, you would work with subject matter specialists to review and analyse the job analysis data. Because the process involves clearly defining the prerequisite knowledge and skills and the additional knowledge/skills required, it is usually conducted in a group focus interview. Once agreement has been reached on the job requirements, then you can go ahead with the development of training.

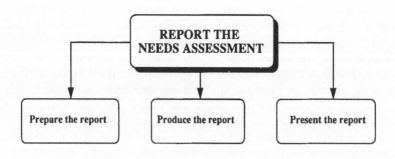

Figure 2.10 *Report the needs assessment*

Report the needs assessment

The client and your management should be kept informed and in touch with developments throughout the needs assessment. They will not want public surprises, especially disagreeable ones, so keep them up to date, discuss progress and give advance notice of the report and any potential problems. At no point should the client or your management be able to say, 'We didn't know that', or 'We didn't want you to follow that plan'. The results of your work will more easily be accepted if management feel they have been kept informed and consulted on the assessment and its progress.

Prepare the report

You need to put almost as much thought and effort into the presentation of your report as into the assessment itself. A good assessment but a poor report generally result in nothing being done and the presenters and their study lose credibility. When you are preparing your report you should:

■ Consider your audience. Who will read this report? What do they need to know? Is the report constructive in tone? Is the audience prepared for the results? How can you best prepare them? What are their reactions likely to be? What will be your responses?
■ Select your reporting methods. How can you best address this particular audience? How long should the report be? What visuals – charts, tables, graphs – will be useful? Will a formal oral presentation be necessary? If so, what back-up information might you require?

Produce the report

The purpose of a needs assessment report is to communicate to management so that they can decide on and implement a course of action. The goal then is to persuade them to do something. Any written report should therefore be in clear simple English and aim to communicate its recommendations powerfully. It might consist of:

■ An executive summary, between two and five pages long. This is probably the most important part of the report because management may read only this. The summary should set out to answer the 'Why', 'How', 'What' and 'What should we do?' questions that management will want answered. It might contain:
  – a brief statement of the situation or problem that gave rise to the needs assessment. Here you are concerned with *why* the needs assessment was conducted;
  – a brief statement of the methods you used to gather information. Here you deal with *'How?'*;

- a summary of the assessment findings. Here the focus should be on the facts of the situation; do not dilute the impact of these by presenting too many opinions. This summary will explain *what* you found out. Try to represent these findings visually through charts, tables and graphs;
- conclusions and recommendations. This section might include possible training options, recommendations and/or a proposed action plan. You need to let management know the advantages and disadvantages of each particular training option, recommendation or plan and how much it will cost. This is the *'What should we do?'* section.

■ Introduction and background. This explains how the report is organized and lets the reader know the history that led up to the needs assessment.

■ Method(s). This describes how the needs assessment was carried out and the reasons for the method or methods used. In this section you might also list the people involved in helping you carry out the assessment.

■ Findings. These should be numbered so that they can be reviewed and referred to more easily.

■ Discussion. This would include a discussion of the implications of the findings for the development of training. Various training options might be considered.

■ Recommendations. Again these should be numbered so that they can be reviewed and referred to more easily. Training recommendations should be clearly worded, point to definite actions and include time/date references where possible. The organizations/people responsible for these actions should also be given.

■ Appendices. These provide supporting documentation and statistical data. Include here material like organization charts, job descriptions, task outlines, survey documents, graphs, charts and any questionnaires you used in the assessment.

Once your report is produced, have someone else read it to 'nit-pick' and look at it from other perspectives. Proof-read the report for accuracy and check spelling, dates, statistics and make sure the numbers add up. In particular, you should check for typographical errors and ask someone else to look for the 'typos'. The packaging of the report or the presentation is also important in terms of credibility and client or management acceptance. You should put the report in an attractive binder and wherever possible use visuals like flowcharts, pie charts, or graphs to highlight and reinforce your points.

Present the report

If there is to be an oral presentation of the report, have a rehearsal or *dry-run* first. You might use a variety of techniques in presenting the results and good overhead transparencies or slides can greatly contribute to the effectiveness of the presentation (see Chapter 4 for more information on how to develop visual aids). At the dry-run invite your colleagues to put themselves in the position of your audience and ask difficult questions. As a result of these questions and your colleagues' comments, you can decide what back-up materials you will need to support your points and recommendations.

Bad news is generally not welcome and you should present it in a clear, factual and constructive way. It needs to be presented diplomatically with positive and practical recommendations for remedying the situation. Enhance any strong points or 'good news' discovered during the assessment and try to finish on a positive note. Indeed, the tone throughout the report should be sympathetic, helpful and honest.

Project Action Items: Assessing training needs in your organization

1. Imagine you are going to train someone to do *your* job. List the things they will need to know. Then list the things they will need to be able to do.

Need to know:_____

_____

Need to do: _____

_____

2. Interview at least three people working at different levels in your organization to obtain information about training needs. Use Figure 2.6 or a similar form for the interviews.

3. Carry out a task analysis using the form below.

TASK BREAKDOWN SHEET

Task:_____   _____

Equipment: _____   _____

Outcome: _____

STAGES	KEY POINTS
List the stages or steps in the job or process.	*Anything in a stage which might affect quality, safety or make the work easier. Include any special information.*
1.	
2.	
3.	
4.	
5.	
6.	
7.	
8.	

3

How to design a training course for active learning

In this chapter we will look at how to design and develop a training course to fit the specific needs of your client and the training population. The key to effective course design is to focus on relevant 'need to know' knowledge and skills and to develop activities for participant involvement. This chapter will focus on ways you can do this and ensure that participants are active rather than passive learners.

Developing a new course is creative work but it needs to be systematic as well. A wealth of creativity in course development without a guiding system may produce lots of interesting experiences, but effective training will not be one of them. On the other hand, an elaborate systems approach without flair or inspiration will produce routine, lack-lustre courses which fail to motivate and engage participants in the learning experience. As we saw in Chapter 1, learning is something people choose to do themselves – the learner controls the switch that makes learning happen. The work of the course developer therefore is not only to provide relevant information for course participants, but to create a motivating, learning environment and stimulating training activities within the framework of a systematic approach.

Inevitably, course development situations differ. They differ in terms of the setting, the client and his or her requirements, the size and needs of the target population, the time available for the training and in many other important respects. Course development certainly does not take place in the ideal world of textbook models and flowcharts. However, a model or system for course development provides a consistent and principled approach to each new project and enables you to get to grips with it from the beginning. A systems approach also ensures that:

■ The overall task and time-scales are clear from the beginning. You do not get unduly delayed with a particular step or activity.

- Everyone involved in course development is 'singing from the same sheet' – knows what their responsibilities are and what comes next. Developers can therefore work relatively independently and new people joining the team can become productive more quickly.
- Different modules or parts of the course can be developed in conjunction with each other, rather than one at a time as in a relay race. This concurrent approach can dramatically reduce the *cycle time*, from beginning the course development to the end.
- Course development is done thoroughly and no important steps are missed out. Developers receive clear direction and can use the model or system as a checklist or job aid.
- Management can see clearly where you are in the course development process and what you are doing. Course development is expensive both in time and money; it requires a logical and systematic approach in order to justify the expense.

Real situations demand flexibility and compromise. In particular, clients and your management are looking for least time/least cost solutions – they often require that courses should be developed quickly and conducted with minimum disruption to the operation. Developers are then obliged to take creative 'short-cuts' – condense the time spent in collecting information, reduce the course length, divide it into separate modules, use off-the-shelf materials rather than develop more appropriate materials of their own, etc. The course development system outlined below is flexible. It offers guidelines rather than a comprehensive prescription. The time taken for each step depends on your own situation and the system can be used by one individual working in a school, college, or training department, or by a larger team.

Initiate course design and development

This is the first step and one generally taken by the training supervisor or project

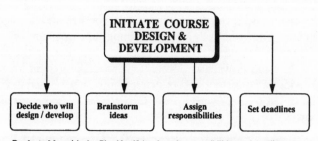

Product : Memo/ Action Plan identifying the task, responsibilities, and deadlines

Figure 3.1 *Initiate course design and development*

leader. It involves using all the information gathered so far from the client, the target population, the needs survey and other sources. It also involves looking at constraints in terms of time, manpower, money and other resources. The course development situation needs to be clarified for everyone concerned: the client, your management and any other people involved in the project. The following four steps are essential.

Decide who will design and develop the course

This may have been decided earlier but at the beginning of the development stage it makes sense to take stock again. The needs survey may have been done by one person but generally development requires more than one. Even an experienced course developer benefits greatly from the different perspectives, ideas and suggestions of others. One person may develop the course but should receive input from others. Joint or small team efforts are often most effective, especially where the knowledge, experience and skills of the developers *complement* each other. The developers may then brainstorm and bounce ideas off each other and the excitement of this often contributes to a stimulating course.

When there is a need for a long training course, or a course requires a great deal of needs assessment and research, large development teams are sometimes set up. There are however great dangers in this. Too large a team may give rise to poor communication and conflict; the team leader may find most of the time taken up in 'coordinating', running meetings, attempting to smooth the waters and reporting to management. Team members may refuse to take responsibility, to 'own' the course, and there is often a fatal lack of accountability. A course put together by a large team may also lack cohesion and appear as a jumble of modules. Rather than saving time by having a lot of people working together, it often takes much longer to develop the training. Worse, as far as management is concerned, large teams are expensive and a costly failure can seriously undermine the credibility of a training group. Finally, as mentioned earlier, some creativity and flair are necessary for effective course development – committees and bureaucracies are not noted for these qualities. Even large projects are best handled by a small team with other people assisting where necessary and acting as subject specialists.

Brainstorm ideas

Brainstorming is a technique which can be used at critical points in course development, particularly when there is need for creativity. In particular, you can use brainstorming at the beginning of a project to collect as many ideas as possible about your approach, course content, the activities and participants' possible reactions. Basically the technique is to:

■ Gather a small group of people who have experience or interest in the course topic. Do not limit the group to those who are already working on the project.

■ Explain that the purpose of the brainstorming session is to generate as many creative suggestions and ideas as possible to help with course development.

■ Emphasize that the need is for creativity and no evaluative remarks – critical or humorous – should be made initially about any of the suggestions. Ideas need to be generated as quickly as possible, to be explored in depth later in the session.

■ Briefly outline the course topic, objectives and background. Do not give too much detail, or you might shut out some good ideas.

■ Ask for suggestions and ideas about how to accomplish the goals of this training – course content, activities, how to interest participants' etc.

■ Encourage the group to be as creative and imaginative as possible.

■ List as many ideas as possible on a flipchart or board which everyone can see. Refuse to select or judge the ideas prematurely.

■ Use your own or other people's ideas as a springboard.

■ Stop when you feel you have enough ideas to choose from; when fresh ideas seem to have dried up; or when participants feel ready to stop.

■ Go through the list of ideas and suggestions, discussing their advantages and disadvantages in terms of practicality, interest, time and all the other relevant factors. Here you begin to select and develop some of the suggestions and ideas for use in the actual training.

Brainstorming is a technique that works well whether you are developing a course by yourself or working with one or more people. If you're working by yourself, try to get one or two other people to discuss the training with you. Brainstorming tends to make the process of course development more stimulating: the developers can work better together and the resulting course is thus made more attractive. Moreover, brainstorming can save a lot of time and money – a great number of interesting and usable ideas can be produced in a short amount of time.

Assign responsibilities

If more than one person is involved in course development, the supervisor or project leader needs to assign responsibilities. The brainstorming session can provide some guidance here. Who wanted to research this topic? Who wanted to use video? Who was interested in using role-plays? Generally the supervisor or project leader should play to people's strengths and interests – ask them to do the things they are good at or interested in. But this is also an opportunity to consider developmental tasks; the person who usually develops the presentation elements might be given responsibility for the practice activities this time; the 'activities' person might work on the presentation material. The attitude should be 'Let's do something new!'. If course development is stimulating for the developers, it is likely that the final training will stimulate participants.

Set deadlines

It is vital for *realistic* deadlines to be established at the beginning. Wishful thinking and over-optimism have led to the failure of many projects. Build in time for unforeseen delays or 'slippage' so that there is some flexibility and management are not 'surprised' by a failure to meet previously established deadlines. The supervisor and developer(s) should discuss and agree on critical dates eg, dates for the *dry-run*, sending out nomination letters and pre-course information, the date of the pilot presentation. Everyone involved should know what the deadlines are and the consequences if these are not met.

Once the task is discussed and defined in this way, then the supervisor can send a brief action plan or memo to each person involved. This plan or memo might briefly identify the task, individual responsibilities and the deadlines. This written record can serve as a guide and control document through the course development. A sample action plan for the development and delivery of an induction programme was shown in Chapter 2, Figure 2.4.

Identify objectives

This is perhaps the most important step in course development and one with which everyone has difficulty. Robert Mager, the *guru* of instructional objectives, defines an objective as:

a description of a performance you want learners to be able to exhibit before you consider them competent. An objective describes an intended *result* of instruction, rather than the *process* of instruction itself (1991).

That first sentence emphasizes the need for learner performance and the demonstration of knowledge or skills. The second sentence serves as a warning to the course developer and to the trainer – the focus should not be on what *you* want to do, the topics *you* want to cover, but on the learners and the results of the

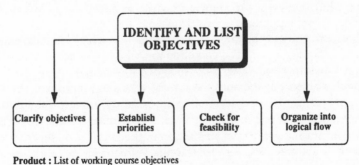

Product : List of working course objectives

Figure 3.2 *Identify and list objectives*

instruction. Novice developers tend to see course development as a matter of deciding what *they* will cover, the content of *their* training. Participant activities are largely an afterthought. The experienced developer, however, focuses on participant objectives and therefore on participant learning activities. The focus is on what the participants will be experiencing, thinking and doing at different points. Participant objectives are also important because:

■ They guide the course developer in the selection and development of information, materials and activities. In particular, objectives force you to think seriously about what is worth teaching and what is worth spending time, effort and money on accomplishing.

■ They direct you in your presentation of the training. Unforeseen incidents may arise, changes need to be made, but the objectives can continue to provide focus and direction for your course and for participants.

■ Objectives focus on participant performance and help them organize their own learning efforts. If at the beginning of the course participants know what's expected of them, they are more inclined and better equipped to work purposefully to achieve the objectives. The participants will make a presentation, write a report, demonstrate a skill. Such objectives make the course more challenging and emphasize that active involvement is required.

■ Objectives provide a means of evaluating the success of the training. The course developer, the trainer, the participant, the participant's supervisor and management all have a means of assessing the value of the course. Did the participant achieve these objectives?

There are three elements in an objective:

1. *Performance*: this is the main element and describes what the participants will be able to do as a result of the training. When you are working on your performance objectives avoid vague verbs like understand, learn, think, know, appreciate, enjoy, discover. Use precise action verbs instead. For knowledge objectives use verbs like identify, classify, describe, state, list, name, define. For skill objectives or when you require participants to apply something use verbs like prepare, produce, evaluate, assemble, install, demonstrate, present, measure, explain.

2. *Condition*: this may be the 'cue' for the task – 'given a materials request' or ' given a faulty engine'. The condition may also be the equipment, materials or manuals that employees will use to perform the task.

3. *Standard*: you can measure the results of training more effectively if you specify standards – the level of speed, accuracy, or acceptability that you expect the employees to reach by the end of training. If you have no standard or your standard is 'to the satisfaction of the manager or supervisor', think carefully about the level of speed, accuracy, frequency, or other qualities you want. Then let your participants know the standard in your statement of the objective(s).

When you have identified your objective(s) ask yourself: 'Am I being too ambitious? Is there enough time for employees to practise and to achieve these objective(s)?'. If you have several objectives, it might be best to deal with them in separate training sessions. If you have one broad objective, you should break it down into several specific objectives which again might be dealt with in several training sessions. Trainers are often tempted to use too many objectives. The basic rule is to have a small number of objectives and ensure that they are achieved.

When you have written your objectives, check their quality. Badly written objectives refer to:

- What the trainer is going to do, rather than what the participant will do.
- Methods the trainer will use rather than what the participants will accomplish.
- Impressive-sounding achievements that are vague in meaning. The best objectives identify participant performance and are written in simple clear English.

Clarify the objectives

If you do not identify and clarify your objectives, then sooner or later there will be confusion: in the course development; in the delivery of the course; among the learners; in the follow-up after the course; or in making an evaluation. You will not really know what you are trying to achieve, nor will the participants be sure of what is expected of them. Your client may well feel justified in saying the training was a waste of time.

But clarification of objectives is easier said than done. It would be convenient if course development neatly followed instructional systems flowcharts, objectives were finalized at the beginning of the project and we logically progressed, step by step. Course development however, like most things in real life and learning, is less mechanical and rather more messy than that.

The identification and clarification of objectives is a process which begins with the needs survey, continues through course development and may not end until after the pilot presentation. At particular points in the development you may feel the need to clarify the objectives once more; after the *dry-run* and pilot presentation, you may feel that certain objectives are not really significant or feasible and choose to concentrate on others.

Certainly you should try to identify and clarify the objectives before course development begins, but you should regard them as *working objectives* rather than final ones carved in stone. These working objectives may well need to be reduced in number, modified, clarified and sharpened, as development makes you more aware of what is feasible with this target population and within the training period.

Establish Priorities

Your needs survey should have identified:

- What problems the client wants to be solved.
- What results the client wants the training to achieve.
- What the participants require – the knowledge and skills they need and want to gain from the course.
- What might be achieved within the constraints of the situation.

At this stage you may have a number of possible objectives.

Knowledge objectives eg, the client might want participants to be presented with information about a new job, procedure, or equipment.
Skill objectives eg, the client may say, 'We want them to operate this machine and do this job'.
Attitudinal objectives eg, the client may say, 'Staff are resisting these new procedures. They need to change their attitudes'.

The first thing you should do is to establish priorities. What do the learners *need* to know and be able to do? Which of these objectives are *nice* to know and be able to do? If learners have attended a course on demonstration skills, they *need* to be able to make clear demonstrations – the training succeeds or fails on that. It would be *nice* if participants improved their use of visual aids as well but that is not the focus of the course. Only when we have achieved the *need to know* objectives should we move on to the *nice to know*.

Check for feasibility

The next question is whether you can achieve these objectives with this target population and within the time limits for the course. Which objectives can you achieve? Which should you make a start on eg, this objective may be too important to leave out but there is insufficient time to accomplish it. One of the major problems here is that knowledge objectives are fairly easy to achieve and do not take much time – 'Just tell them', some clients say 'and give them a test'. Skill objectives take longer because practice and a degree of mastery is required. Although you may not have enough time for participants to master a skill, you can usually provide sufficient practice for them to achieve basic competence. Attitudinal objectives are even more time-consuming because they involve changing people's viewpoints and you can expect some resistance. Quite often you do not have the luxury of that time but you can at least make a start. Discussion and structured experiences like role play and simulations can be effective in influencing people or at least break the crust of entrenched views and attitudes.

Organize objectives into a logical flow

Important questions here are:

- 'What are the prerequisites for this training?', and 'What do our participants know already about this topic, and what skills do they already have?'.

■ 'Which objective comes first?', 'Do participants need to achieve *this* objective before they can work towards the others?'.

Answers to the first question should help you establish where to start and what should be the first objective. Answers to the second question should help build up a hierarchy of objectives – participants need to know or be able to do *this* before they can do *this*.

We tend to place knowledge objectives first – participants will need this information and these guidelines before they can do anything. The danger here though is that you may spend too much time on knowledge objectives and leave insufficient practice time. Indeed practice is the element most frequently missing from courses and lack of relevant guided practice is probably the main reason for failures in training. Participants know about the task or skill but are unable to perform. For example, management training courses often tell participants how to make decisions, lead meetings, or coach employees but provide insufficient structured practice to rehearse, test or modify the theory. Participants go back to their jobs and the 'learning' does not transfer – the theory and the training are discredited.

All too often then, the course developer or the trainer claims that there is not enough time for practice in a course. The trainer's focus however should be on achieving limited and necessary objectives and reducing the amount of content and *nice to know* information.

The final product of this stage should be a brief list of working objectives. In practice it is best to choose no more than three or four objectives for a one-day course. These are enough for participants to focus on and if each objective is significant, it will take time to accomplish. Longer courses may necessarily have more objectives.

Collect information and materials

There are a variety of sources you can use to collect course information and materials; these are given below:

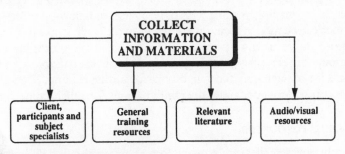

Product : File of course resource materials

Figure 3.3 *Collect relevant information and materials*

Clients, participants and subject specialists

You can follow-up on the needs survey and gain additional information from the client and potential participants. A subject specialist can also serve as a continuing source of information and a possible resource in the course presentation; for example, he or she could be available to answer detailed or technical questions during a question and answer session. By consulting with the client, the potential participants and the subject specialist you not only gain more information but make them more interested, more involved and more committed to the success of the training. Indeed the involvement of user groups in the development of a course is the best way of building support for training.

General training resources

Prior to full-scale course development, you should find out what other courses are available on this topic. Avoid reinventing the wheel! You need to review similar or relevant training courses and ask yourself: 'What's applicable?', 'What can be adapted to our specific circumstances?', 'Will this material help us achieve our training objectives?'. You might review training resource books such as the annual *Developing Human Resources* handbook which provides different types of group activity, case studies, questionnaires and lecturettes on common training topics. Training magazines like the British *Training and Development* journal, the American *Training and Development Journal* and *Training* also provide a wealth of information and activities, some of which may be relevant to your own particular course topic and objectives. Publishers like Kogan Page also produce workshop packages on general topics like communications skills, project management and team building (see the list of References and Further Resources at the back of this book).

Relevant literature

Your research can provide background and potential training material – content for the presentation elements in the course, or resource material for activities. Company information, brief readings or articles can be included in a participant handbook, as pre-reading, reading within the course, or follow-up reading. Written questions can be used to focus on key points in the reading, guide participants and structure and focus any discussion. When course development has involved a great amount of research and readings are included in the handbook, staff often appreciate a list of references and suggestions for further reading. Such a list also credits the course developer and trainer with having 'done their homework'.

Audio-visual resources

You not only need to collect additional information but also find different means of presenting the course content. It has long been recognized that the use of audio-visual aids – film, video, slides, slide tape – adds variety to a training session, provides a change of activity and pace and generally increases the effectiveness of learning. Speakers using visual aids are perceived as being better prepared, more professional, clearer, more interesting and more concise than speakers who do not use visuals. This applies not only to business and sales presentations but to training presentations as well. Indeed, participants in training sessions now *expect* film, video, or slides and a course without an audio-visual component tends to be considered boring or amateur. There is a wealth of a/v material available for training purposes, and if you can not find something appropriate, it may be possible to produce something of your own which is both effective and relatively inexpensive (see Chapter 4).

A final product of your research and materials collection is a file of resources. This should not only provide you with materials directly for the course, but back-up information, additional activities and support.

Develop content, practice and application activities

We usually divide courses into modules of instruction with one module for each objective. Each individual module then consists of:

1. The module objective.
2. The information needed for accomplishing the objective.
3. Practice or application activities – activities through which participants assimilate the course content, practice and apply the knowledge or skill.
4. Feedback or evaluation of the learning – activities in which the trainer and participants check whether the module objective has been achieved.

This modular approach to course development allows revisions to be made and implemented more quickly as circumstances and, accordingly, objectives change. It also allows for the development of courses which consist of *common core modules* (appropriate for everyone's needs) plus *customized modules* (appropriate for a particular department or organization's needs). For example, a course on on-the-job training(OJT) may consist of several common core modules plus a department-specific module dealing with a department's own training programme. In the same way, the information presented in a course on, for example project management, may be *generic* but the activities and exercises customized to fit a particular job or department's needs.

Develop activities

The development of content and practice activities involves the following steps.

Select and sequence content
Here you decide what information is necessary for accomplishing the objective

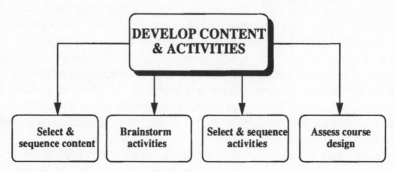

Product : Outline of content and activities

Figure 3.4 *Develop content and appliation activities*

and in what order it should be presented. Based on the objective, you need to discriminate between what participants *need* to know and what is *nice* to know. If time is short, then only *need to know* information should be presented. *Information overload* – the presentation of more information than the participant can absorb at one time, is a constant danger. This is particularly true of induction or introductory courses where trainers sometimes think they have to transmit as much information as possible in the shortest possible time.

As far as sequencing of content is concerned, you must decide what information will be included in the introduction, the presentation, the application/practice activities and the concluding activities. The usual sequencing criteria – familiar to unfamiliar, simple to complex, easy to difficult, first step to last in a process or skill – usually provide an order of content. Take account of interest and motivation factors however; a slightly challenging or difficult activity near the beginning of the course may stimulate participant interest.

Decide who or what will present the course content. Alternatives to the trainer providing all the input are: the participants (perhaps we can elicit some of this information from them); the media (readings, video, film); or structured experiences like case studies and role-plays. A variety of content delivery systems is desirable in order to provide an interesting course and one which actively engages participants in learning. Even well-motivated participants will struggle if the course mainly consists of the trainer speaking. The *information – activity – reporting* cycle is a useful one to follow.

Clarity of content is also a major concern. A logical progression of ideas, appropriate examples, clear visual aids, time for participants to assimilate/discuss/apply the information, a well-organized participant handbook – all these contribute to the clarity of the course. Most important of all however, the language level of the presentation and of the materials should be appropriate for the target population. Technical or training jargon should be avoided and unless you have a roomful of experts sitting in front of you, follow the KISS principle – Keep It Short and Simple.

Brainstorm practice activities

Clients are often like novice teachers or course developers in their concern for transmitting as much content, as much information as possible, to the target population. Practice and application, however, are vital if people are effectively to use and apply new knowledge or skills. Sometimes the practice/application activities required are fairly obvious, particularly in skills training. A course on demonstration techniques should provide practice in giving demonstrations; one on using a new computer program should provide hands-on practice with the program; a course on effective team meetings obviously involves participants in team meetings. But you still need to design and develop these practice /application activities; and then what activities do you provide for more 'general' training – a staff induction course, an interpersonal skills course, or training for new supervisors?

One way of generating ideas for practice/application activities is to have another brainstorming session. Everyone involved comes together, reviews the current status of course development and tackles the issue of how best to achieve the training objectives through practice activities. At this stage the brainstormers should try to think through and experience the course as participants: if you were a participant and needed to achieve these objectives, what activities would motivate you, what things would you need or want to do? List as many ideas as possible, try to be imaginative and use each others' ideas as a springboard. When you have sufficient ideas, then you can develop the practice activities. Another advantage of brainstorming again is that it brings the developers together at a critical stage, gives an opportunity for them to review progress and stimulates them to contribute new ideas.

Select and sequence activities

Take the results of the brainstorming session and select and sequence the possible course activities. Figure 3.5 shows a list of common activities. Notice how they are sequenced. Those activities where the learning materials come from sources outside the participants (books, articles, media, company material, etc.) and which are mainly directed by the trainer have been listed first. As you go down through the list, the activities are increasingly participant-centred with more opportunity for discovery learning and individual responses.

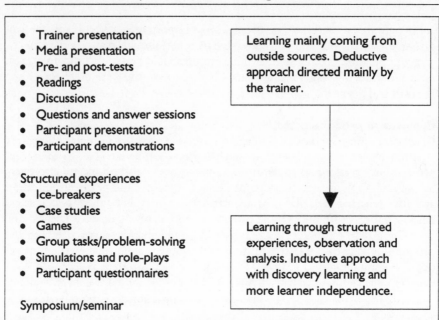

- Trainer presentation
- Media presentation
- Pre- and post-tests
- Readings
- Discussions
- Questions and answer sessions
- Participant presentations
- Participant demonstrations

Structured experiences
- Ice-breakers
- Case studies
- Games
- Group tasks/problem-solving
- Simulations and role-plays
- Participant questionnaires

Symposium/seminar

Learning mainly coming from outside sources. Deductive approach directed mainly by the trainer.

Learning through structured experiences, observation and analysis. Inductive approach with discovery learning and more learner independence.

Figure 3.5 *List of common training activities*

Training activities

The list of training activities in Figure 3.5 above does not claim to be exhaustive. Perhaps you can add some of your own and locate them in the learning range. However, we will examine these common course activities in more detail.

Trainer presentation

As suggested earlier, we generally need to reduce content presentation time and increase practice or application time. Participants can sometimes feel cheated of the information they want however, especially those who prefer a direct 'tell it to me' style and who want to hear the 'expert'. This problem occurs particularly in developing countries where classrooms are teacher-centred and students tend to be passive and dependent on the teacher. Obviously the trainer should not efface him or herself and deny valuable input to the participants. On the other hand, consider the ratio of trainer talk or activity to participant talk or activity. Who is getting all the practice? The course developer should, if possible, break down a long presentation into several short ones and ensure that visual reinforcement or relief is provided.

Media Presentation

Video, film and slides can be used to present course information. An important point here though is to avoid the 'television' response where participants sit back to enjoy the show. Make the viewing interactive through the use of pre-viewing questions, worksheets or tasks. These help participants focus on important information, force them to think and provide a structure for any subsequent discussion.

Pre- and post- tests

A pre-test provides you with information on what the participants already know or can do. It lets participants know what the course will focus on, what is expected of them and increases the motivation to succeed. If, in their post-test, participants significantly improve on their pre-test score or performance, they often leave feeling the training has been very successful. Pre- and post-tests are most effective though when the course objectives are mainly knowledge objectives, the pre-test is scored by the participants themselves and therefore a low score is non-threatening.

Readings

A reading may be sent to participants as preparation for a training session; assigned during the actual course as preparation or reinforcement for an activity; or given as follow-up reading. Reading assignments can provide participants with necessary background information, specific examples and case studies. These reading assignments should be chosen very carefully though, to include only highly relevant readings which should be kept short and, if necessary, abridged. To make the assignment even more effective and also ensure that it is done, provide tasks or questions on the reading. These oblige participants to focus on specific information in the reading and to apply the information to their own situation. Based on the task or questions, there can then be a discussion of the reading and its application. Adequate time needs to be provided for the actual reading and completion of the questions. If pre-course reading is assigned, it is a good idea to provide participants with time to 'review' the reading and the task or questions before the discussion or other activity starts. It is surprising how many people may not have had 'time' to do the reading before the course. It can also be very embarrassing if you 'discover' those people who were 'too busy'.

Discussions

Discussions are often used at different stages in a course and for a variety of purposes. There are two main types of discussion:

1. *Formal structured discussions* which are included in the agenda or trainer's presentation outline. These discussions are usually structured by oral or written questions and may involve the completion of a task or worksheets.
2. *Informal feedback discussions* which may be held at any time during the training to check participant understanding and encourage involvement. These informal feedback discussions depend on how the trainer feels things

are progressing and on the time available. (Informal discussions are dealt with in more detail in Chapter 5).

This chapter on course design deals with formal structured discussions and the most common types are discussed below.

Start-up discussions. These can be used at the beginning of a course when participants introduce themselves. You might use a *starting question* to get participants involved right away, find out how much they know on a topic and what their attitudes are. For example, in a course on team-building you might ask participants individually about their experience of working in teams. Such questions often draw out any *hidden agendas* and enable you to make necessary adjustments to the course or to your training style.

Focus Group Technique. This is another way in which you can use discussion at the beginning of a course to identify problem areas and neutralize any participant hostility. You might ask participants to write down their three main concerns related to the course topic. After they have written these down, you can ask each person in turn for their points and list them on the flipchart or board. This technique is rather like brainstorming and there should be no discussion while the concerns are being identified. Once they have been listed however, participants can decide which are the most important and which they can do something about. Possible ways of dealing with these issues are discussed and here you might relate the concerns to the objectives, material and activities in the course. If the needs survey and the research were done thoroughly, there should be a reasonable 'fit' and you can address any residual concerns before the end of the course.

Discussion of readings/film/video. These discussions may be structured by oral and/or written questions. A mixture of *closed* and *open* questions is often most effective. The closed questions will require the correct retrieval of information from the reading, film or video. The open questions will require participants to select and apply information thus gained to their own job situations. You might distribute question sheets for participants to work on individually, in pairs or groups. Then the answers can be discussed.

Discussions can take up a lot of time. The developer needs to budget realistically for any formal discussion activity because participants hate to feel they have been cut off in the middle of an exciting session. During the *dry-run* or rehearsal for the first presentation of the course, you should check discussion activities for clarity of task and how much time is needed for an adequate discussion of the topic.

Question and answer session

If the training session is designed as an induction for new staff or to introduce a new system or project, then it is particularly important to provide for question and answer sessions. When participants are actively involved in the implementation of something new, they need time for questions and discussion. Indeed, they may have some good ideas and suggestions for improvements! A specialist who has been involved with the new system or project may assist here. There are several advantages to this, but also some dangers. Important advantages are that the specialist can answer technical and detailed questions, receive feedback from participants and also make better contact with people implementing the new system or project.

As a trainer though, you need to be aware of the dangers and 'know' your specialist. Some specialists are not skilled in making presentations and, unless you prepare them adequately, can create confusion. Specialists may also lack skill in responding to participants. Staff naturally question and some may resist a new system or project; the defensive or angry reactions of an 'expert' may create additional hostility and you might be forced to intervene. Knowing how your specialist performs, you may choose to predict possible questions and obtain the necessary information yourself. If there are any questions you can not answer, or participants want more details, you can give the specialist's phone number.

Participant presentations/demonstrations

In multiple-day courses short presentations by participants can be used at the beginning of the day to review the previous day's learning. Participant demon-

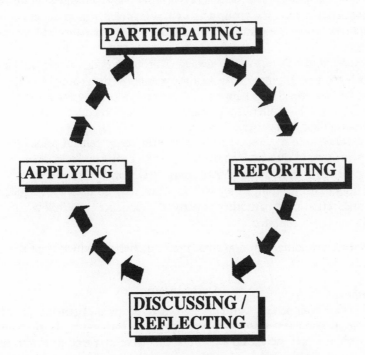

Figure 3.6 *Structured experiences: learning cycle*

strations may also be used in a course beginning with a model demonstration by the trainer and/or media; then the participants demonstrate. Feedback on participant presentations or demonstrations can be given through group discussion, videotape replay, or the use of checklists.

Structured experiences

A structured experience provides a framework for *learning through the experience of an activity*. In other words, structured experiences involve learning through discovery, observation and analysis. This is *inductive learning*, proceeding from experience and observation, in contrast to *deductive learning*, proceeding from general ideas that we usually gain from readings and trainer or media presentations.

Almost any activity that involves self-assessment or group interaction can be used as a structured experience. Most structured experiences however take the form of a group task or problem-solving activity. Structured experiences involve the learning cycle shown in Figure 3.6.

Let us look in more detail at these stages in the structured experience:

1. *Participating in the activity*. Activities that involve self-assessment or pair/group interaction may be used.
2. *Reporting the activity*. The focus here is on *what* happened and what the results of the activity were. If a group activity was involved, group leaders or representatives report the results of the activity and participants add their comments.
3. *Discussing and reflecting on the activity*. This involves discussing the patterns of behaviour and communication, the dynamics of the group. Here the focus is on *how* and *why* things happened. Previously selected *observers* may be used to report and the trainer uses probing questions to encourage participants to reflect on their experience.
4. *Generalizing and applying*. The trainer elicits some general principles from participants and then adds to them. This process naturally leads on to planning for more effective behaviour in the 'real world'. This may involve participants in listing things they will do when they go back to the job, or in writing action plans. Another structured experience may follow this stage and the cycle is repeated.

The following are some common structured experiences, which were shown in Figure 3.5.

Ice-breakers

Ice-breakers are designed to 'warm up' a group of people and generate an interest in learning. Ice-breakers introduce participants to each other, help create the climate within which the group will work and serve as a lead-in to the course topic. They also give the trainer an opportunity to see 'who' is in the group and how the group functions together.

Here are some key points to consider when you develop or choose an ice-breaker:

■ The activity should interest people. You need to override participants' thoughts about work, home problems or the traffic that morning and ensure they are mentally as well as physically present. Participants may ignore the instructor, but it's very difficult for them to ignore fellow participants when they are involved in an exercise that requires them to reach a goal.

■ An ice-breaker should initiate networking. The longer a course is, the more important networking becomes. An ice-breaker that starts people networking eliminates their concerns about fitting in and making a contribution.

■ An ice-breaker should be relevant to the course. You need to avoid a situation where busy employees complete the ice-breaker and think, 'Well that was fun. But what's the point? We're not here for entertainment'. There are a variety of possible icebreakers including:

 – An introductory question, which the trainer might write up on the flip-chart and use to elicit participants' information, experience and some indication of their attitudes towards the course topic. For example, at the start of a trainer training programme the question, 'What are the charac-teristics of an effective trainer?' might be discussed.

 Introductory questions can also be used with large audiences to increase involvement and interaction at the beginning of a seminar or symposium. The audience can be asked to turn to two or three of their neighbour(s), introduce themselves and discuss a specific question. For example, 'What are the main problems facing us in...?'. Participants might discuss this for a few minutes and then the trainer can elicit and write up key responses on the flipchart.

 – Short interviews between participants. The trainer might provide two or three minutes for each interview and a list of interview questions for participants to use. Participants might even choose to add to these ques-tions. Here is an ice-breaker used before a presentation on adult learning.

The purpose of this exercise is to discover the resources of the people in our group, particu-larly as they relate to adult learning. You must interview your fellow participants. Have them put their name in the space provided once you have matched them up with the appropriate items below:

Find two people to tell you about one of their best learning experiences and why they felt it was so good.

Find two people who learned something in the past week. How did they learn it – through reading, watching something, trying something out, etc.

Find two people who can explain or can show you mind mapping.

Another lively variation on the interview technique is shown in the ice-breaker activity in Figure 3.7. This ice-breaker was developed for a new employee induction course but can be easily adapted to fit other circumstances.

Ice-breakers emphasize the idea that training involves a partnership between the trainer and participants – that participants should not be dependent on the trainer or course material and that everyone's experience and viewpoint has a value.

AUTOGRAPH WORKSHEET

Instructions: During the autograph-hunting session you will interview other participants to find people who fit at least ten of the information areas. For example, you might find someone who has lived in this area for more than 10 years. You then obtain that person's autograph in the appropriate space. You must have a different autograph for each of the ten areas.

	Information area	Autograph
1.	Has lived in this area for more than ten years	
2.	Enjoyed previous job	
3.	Has worked in this business or industry before	
4.	Has more than two children	
5.	Plays golf	
6.	Knows how to use a computer	
7.	Can speak a foreign language	
8.	Has visited the USA	
9.	Can play bridge	
10.	Likes playing or watching football	
11.	Likes to work as part of a team	
12.	Plays a musical instrument	
13.	Lives in the countryside	
14.	Makes a list of Things To Do each day	
15.	Rides a bicycle to work	
16.	Likes to read books	
17.	Has a computer at home	
18.	Has an unusual hobby	
19.	Likes to learn new things	
20.	Has learned something new recently	

Figure 3.7 *Induction ice-breaker*

Case Studies

Case studies place participants in specific work situations and are a popular way to increase participant involvement and job relevance. They are used particularly in supervisory and management training courses to provide practice in the analysis of work situations, in the exercise of judgement and in the definition of appropriate action or solutions. Case studies may range from the large-scale management or business case study to short descriptions of work situations culminating in the question, 'What would you do?'. They can be presented through a description, a collection of 'authentic' documents (as in an *in-basket* exercise), or through a short film or video. The film or video often consists of short vignettes or a sequence of incidents where participants are asked to give their own responses to the situations portrayed. In this way the activity is made interactive, real drama is added and participants get a sense of the emotions that generally go along with real-life situations.

Case studies may be produced externally (as in an *off-the-shelf* training film or video), by the course developer, the trainer, or the participants. The course developer or the trainer can best develop case studies using information gained through the needs survey. Like all group activities though, these case studies should be tested out carefully with colleagues, particularly in the *dry-run*. Alternatively, during the course itself, participants can use their own experience of the job and real-life problems to develop case studies and this increases the relevance and credibility of the course.

Games

One reason for the popularity of games as a training method is that we enjoyed learning from games in our childhood. People learn best when they are engaged in the learning process and games can boost participant interest and involvement. They also offer a welcome change of pace and can generate a light and comfortable atmosphere.

When you begin a course with a game, you break the ice and can introduce the content in an interesting way. This can lower tension and make people comfortable in their new learning environment. Games can provide the data-generating part of a structured experience and are used quite often to explore group dynamics, leadership styles and decision making. For example, a game like Lego Man, which involves teams trying to produce a man made out of Lego pieces, may be used in a variety of ways – to focus on how participants work together in teams, to look at planning and decision-making processes, or to consider leadership or supervisory styles.

All games have an element of competition and are particularly useful in team building. Energy and enthusiasm are generated and become contagious. The interpersonal dynamics of a game also allow the participants to learn something about themselves, how they work with other people and the impact of their behaviour on others.

The process of playing a game needs to be simple so that participants can focus on the content. Games also take time – some might take a day, others only an hour. Quite often course developers underestimate the time needed and this is one of the things you need to check in a *dry-run*. In particular, allow sufficient time to finish the game and to debrief the participants. The debriefing session, which might involve the use of structured observation and participant evaluations, can give participants valuable feedback about their skill levels.

Like other structured experiences, games can seem extremely clever and engaging when you are involved in them. If the instructional effects are trivial however, participants will be irritated and may become cynical about future exercises.

Group tasks/problem solving

Learning in small groups usually involves four to seven participants in each group. Below four, the number of exchanges is often too small to provide a rapid generation of productive ideas; above seven, the number of exchanges is too high to provide satisfactory participation and involvement.

Small group activities are invaluable as a means of maximizing individual practice and the application of learning. In particular, they ensure that participants stay active and involved, and mental and physical cobwebs are not allowed to develop. Group tasks generally result in:

■ a product eg, a video, a working schedule, a plan for a training session;
■ a series of findings or recommendations eg, a list of possible solutions to problems identified earlier in the course; or
■ a decision eg, given a particular job and these candidates (details on each candidate provided) which of them would you select?

The results of the group activity are shown or reported to the other groups. A number of potential group activities like case studies and games have already been mentioned. There are however an infinite variety of possible group activities and a major task in course development is to devise group activities to fit the training topic and objectives.

Simulations and role-plays

Simulations and role-plays can provide participants with direct help in coping with job situations. Videotaping *participant demonstrations* during a course enables trainers to rehearse and improve the job demonstrations they make to their trainees. A team meeting simulation enables the 'supervisor' and the other participants to rehearse the real thing. Clearly these are not the real settings – the participants who follow the trainer's demonstration are not the real trainees, the participants in the team meeting are not the real subordinates. Indeed they are *better* than the real thing – the trainer and the supervisor are practising in a supportive environment and the trainees or the subordinates are less threatening than the real trainees or subordinates might be. If things go wrong in a simulation or role play, participants sometimes say this is not how they would behave in the real situation. Without the supportive environment and sympathetic trainees or subordinates, however, they might well be even worse!

Simulations make change or improvement seem practical, and the focus on skill objectives and practice generally gives participants the sense that they have improved by the end of the training session. In the same way, role-play increases learning through doing, imitation, observation, analysis and feedback. Role-plays are like case studies in action, but whereas the case study provides mainly intellectual involvement, the role-play offers intellectual *and* emotional involvement in a situation. Role-plays therefore can be particularly effective when the objectives involve developing communication skills, interpersonal skills, or changing attitudes. Participants are given opportunities to rehearse different roles, or try new approaches to a role in which previously they may not have been very successful. Role-plays can make the performance of new roles or changes in individual behaviour seem practical – 'I really can conduct an effective performance review'; 'These are some techniques I can use in meetings' or 'I could use this coaching method'. Role-plays therefore can give confidence to the person who needs and wants to develop new skills.

Participant questionnaires

Questionnaires are often used in communications or interpersonal skills training. Participants complete, score and analyse the results of these questionnaires or checklists themselves. The questions may be on learning style, teacher/trainer style, supervisory style or interpersonal communication skills, and a wide variety of questionnaires are available. They often involve participants taking stock of their existing views and attitudes and may be used at the beginning of a course as ice-breakers and to make participants aware of their approach and attitudes to the training topic. The communication skills questionnaire, for example, shown in Figure 3.8 was used at the beginning of a coaching skills workshop.

One advantage of using questionnaires is that people are familiar with them and like to find out about themselves. Questionnaires are particularly useful when you have attitudinal objectives, for the self-awareness that can come through the use of questionnaires is a precondition for changes in attitude. Another important advantage is that when participants get information about their personal style from a questionnaire they've filled in themselves, they are more likely to trust that data as compared with data they receive from the trainer or another person. By *privately* identifying their own style, participants have an opportunity to reflect on it and consider the alternative styles that the questionnaire and the training later will present. The power and the responsibility for change and personal growth therefore lie with them.

When you include structured experiences in a training session you need to provide time for the activities, for discovery learning, processing and application. The trainer-directed and deductive learning approach is more economical in terms of time. The learning gained from structured experiences, however, often

Communication skills

Communication is one of the most important aspects of your job. Coaching in particular is a test of your knowledge about communication and your communication skills. The following questionnaire checks your general knowledge of communication and is intended to make you think about your coaching skills. Indicate whether you think the following statements are true or false,

	Statement	True	False
1.	Communication is a fairly simple process		
2.	If an instruction is clearly understood, it will nearly always be carried out		
3.	People often communicate without realizing it		
4.	Listening well comes natually to most people		
5.	Just listening to problems does little good unless you can offer the person some good advice		
6.	Intelligent people should understand a message the first time		
7.	A person who asks a lot of questions does not understand as clearly as a person who asks only a few questions		
8.	When people do not understand a message, they nearly always tell you so		
9.	Repeating what a person has said is a good check to see if you understood the message properly		
10.	The way a person stands or sits is an important form of communication		
11.	A person's facial expression can change the meaning of the words spoken		
12.	Nodding your head up and down while listening usually indicates interest		
13.	Stating a point loudly and frequently is often the most effective way to make it understood		
14.	A person who really disagrees may say he or she agrees only to avoid further argument		
15.	Effective communication seldom takes place between people who are angry		

Figure 3.8 *Communication skills questionnaire*

has a greater impact on individuals and lasts longer than the learning gained from direct 'teaching'.

Symposium/Seminar

One of the trainer's key roles is as a facilitator and coordinator of training efforts. A symposium or seminar is one way to bring together a variety of 'experts' to discuss an important issue among themselves and with other staff who are involved. You might organize a seminar to:

- publicize a new project or training programme;
- identify and explore a training topic, issue or problem;
- provide a forum for communication and discussion;
- encourage coordination among different departments or groups.

There are a number of advantages to the seminar or symposium format:

■ If you select speakers carefully, all aspects of an issue can be presented and you can provide comprehensive coverage.
■ Frequent changes of speaker and viewpoint can maintain a high interest level.
■ The event can encourage interaction and networking with an involvement activity at the beginning, a question and answer period after each session and a final panel discussion.

JOB TRAINING AND CERTIFICATION SYMPOSIUM

Date: June 10 1995

Time: 09.00–15.30

Venue: Auditorium

AGENDA

09.00–09.15	Symposium opening
09.15–09.45	Overview of National Vocational Qualifications system
09.45–10.15	Management and supervisory roles in training
10.15–10.30	*Break*
10.30–11.15	Job training methods
11.15–12.00	Materials for job training
12.00–13.00	*Lunch*
13.00–14.00	Workplace assessment
14.00–14.15	*Break*
14.15–15.15	Panel discussion: job training and certification
15.15–15.30	Symposium review and action planning

Figure 3.9 *Programme for a training symposium*

Here are some steps to take when you organize a seminar or symposium:

- Identify a theme and objectives for the event.
- Draft an agenda and discuss it with colleagues and others in your organization. Figure 3.9 is a draft agenda for a symposium on the theme of job training and certification.
- Make the logistical arrangements – room reservations, meals, etc.
- Identify potential speakers and obtain approval for their participation. Speakers must be ready to devote time to preparation and should be selected for their ability to communicate and listen to others. They must be concerned to respond to 'the customer' rather than just defend their position or operation. Defensiveness in particular can create problems in question and answer sessions.
- Make sure the speakers are prepared – meet them beforehand to discuss their content, visuals, any questions that may arise. Trouble-shoot the presentation with them and if necessary arrange for a *dry-run*.
- Identify appropriate participants – who needs to be involved, who needs to know about the topic, whose support will be useful.
- If this is a formal symposium, collect and edit the presentation abstracts. Print and distribute the programme and publicity for the event.
- Ask a guest speaker, perhaps someone high up in your organization, to open the seminar/symposium and sum up at the end of the event.
- Distribute a feedback/evaluation form and ask participants for suggestions for future sessions.
- Follow-up. Send thank you letters to the speakers and copy their supervisors. Report on the event to your own management, including the results of the feedback.

Assess the course design

Here are some important factors to bear in mind when selecting and sequencing training activities.

The participants

The needs survey and the work done so far on course development should have provided you with valuable information about the target population. You should know what types and combinations of activities would interest them and get them involved in accomplishing the training objectives. Perhaps even more important, you should know what type of activities would 'turn them off' and prove ineffective. Mature participants with a great deal of information and experience to contribute often prefer discussions, group activities and structured experiences. A course for existing supervisors and managers might use quite a lot of these activities and the trainer would be very much a facilitator. Lecturing such an experienced audience and having them work mainly individually might well create hostility.

A variety of learning styles

Quite often the participants attending a course will have a variety of educational/training backgrounds, attitudes towards learning and learning styles. Considering the target population, the developer needs to provide a variety of activities: listening, discussing, reading, working on a task or problem, practising, demonstrating, role-playing, evaluating. Successful courses not only provide this range of activities but also a variety of formats. Small group, pair, individual and full group activities not only cater to participants' needs for various interactions but to their individual social styles.

Sequence and flow of activities

Make sure there are appropriate breaks and transitions in the course, and move on smoothly and effectively from one activity to another. Here are a few practical questions to consider:

■ When should the coffee breaks occur? Breaks are often scheduled at the end of a presentation or on completion of a group activity. In particular, they can also provide an interval between a small group activity and the groups reporting their results. Breaks need not truncate a group activity however. If participants are really involved in their task, they may choose to get their coffee, come back to the training room and work through the break.

■ What should follow the lunch break? A film, videotape, or a series of slides could lull the participants to sleep and a presentation puts demands on the trainer but not perhaps on the participants. A lively small group activity might be the best choice to ensure that participants are actively involved once more.

■ Do the participants need a brief review at the beginning of the afternoon session? Sometimes this is helpful, but it should not turn into a trainer presentation or trainer-led discussion with only a few people actively involved. Where possible, participants should do the reviewing.

■ In a multiple-day course, do participants need to review the previous day's activities at the beginning of each morning? A daily review is often useful as a means of focusing once more on course or module objectives, eliciting what participants have learnt, or finding out what they may still be unsure of. It is also useful as a means of linking what was learnt 'yesterday' with what will be dealt with 'today'. Participant presentations of something they learned the previous day or prepared for 'homework' can be used to review the previous day's learning.

Timing and pacing of activities

You need to judge how long *this* particular activity will take with *this* target population. How long should it take to complete the task properly? At the course development stage you only need approximate times and to produce a tentative agenda. Firm decisions can be made after the experience of the *dry-run* and the *pilot* provide an opportunity for fine-tuning.

Throughout course development you need to bear in mind the training objectives and the target population's needs or wants. You need to keep asking yourself questions eg, 'What would I think of this course if I were sitting in their place?'; 'Does the course address the target population's needs and wants?'; 'Does this material or activity contribute directly to the achievement of objectives?'; 'Have the objectives been achieved?'. This last question emphasizes the need for feedback and evaluation activities during and at the end of the course. The trainer's use of questioning, the structured and the informal discussions and the reports of group activities provide feedback. More formal means of evaluation – particularly in terms of performance-based training – can be provided by pre- and post-tests, participant demonstrations and those simulation and role-play activities where the participant has to follow set guidelines and meet criteria for success.

Final products of this development stage are a course description, trainer's outline and an agenda for the *dry-run*.

Conduct a dry-run

A *dry-run* is a rehearsal for the first or *pilot* presentation of a course. Like the dress rehearsal for a play, the *dry-run* establishes a deadline, a little before the grand opening, for everything to be ready. It provides a valuable opportunity to bring everything together and try out the new course – not only the content, the activities and instructional methods, but the logistics of conducting this training. The *dry-run* is increasingly common in business training where training departments, like theatre producers, want to ensure that everything will be 'alright on the night' and the production a success.

At a *dry-run* the audience should be your colleagues with the subject specialists or representatives of the client department also attending. Your colleagues know what is involved in developing and presenting a course and can provide the necessary professional help; the representatives of the client department also have

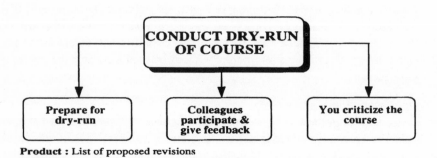

Product : List of proposed revisions

Figure 3.10 *Conduct a dry-run of the course*

Dry-run feedback form

Course title – Introduction to the Company
Requested by – Personnel Department
Target population – New staff who have joined the company in the past month. Most of them are young people who have just left school
Participants per course – 10 to 24
Time, date, and site of dry-run – 1 p.m. on 10 Jan in conference room 2A
Date of pilot presentation – 1 Feb.
Course developer(s) – AMS with JLL and ARS
Course presenter(s) – AMS, JLL
Subject matter specialist(s) – JY and WW from Personnel
Dry-run participants – ARS, TMM, MJT, EM, CB from Training and JY and WW from Personnel. Guests training manager and personnel manager
Length of course – One day   **Length of dry-run** – Three hours
Dry-run comments
Introduction and objectives

_____

Content

_____

Practice activities

_____

Feedback/evaluation activities

_____

Participant materials

_____

Visual aids

_____

Suggestions

_____

Signed _____

Figure 3.11 *Dry-run feedback form*

an opportunity to make some final suggestions and give their department's approval of the course.

In the *dry-run* colleagues 'trouble-shoot' the training from two perspectives – from the perspective of the target population, and from the course developer and trainer's perspective. As participants, they identify potential *hidden agendas* or misconceptions that the target population might bring along with them, raise difficult questions that might be asked and examine the different activities from the participants' perspective. Then from the developer and trainer's perspective they provide feedback suggesting ways of avoiding or overcoming some of these difficulties. They give advice on how the objectives can be clarified and how the content, activities and presentation of the course can be made more effective. One way of organizing this feedback is to provide participants with a *dry-run* feedback sheet like the one in Figure 3.11. Prior to the *dry-run* you can fill in the first part of the form as shown and this will prepare participants for the session.

Prepare for the dry-run

Here you should simulate as closely as possible the actual course preparation. This may involve preparation of:

- Colleagues who are going to attend the *dry-run* eg, giving them the *dry-run* feedback sheet and any pre-course reading materials or tasks.
- Training materials eg, flipchart, overhead transparencies, slides, films, videos, handouts.
- Participant materials eg, handbooks, role-play sheets, performance materials for participants to make a demonstration, presentation, or to produce something.
- Equipment eg, overhead projector, slide projector, film projector, video recorder, camera, etc.
- The room and furniture eg, the table and chairs arrangement, positioning of equipment.

Participation and feedback of colleagues

The important question here is, 'How should feedback be given?'. Obviously it is undesirable for the *dry-run* to get stuck on discussion of one activity or issue, but at the same time you do not want to lose valuable suggestions. One solution is for participants to jot down their comments on the feedback sheet, give oral feedback at the end of each activity and then finally at the end of the course. Participants might raise questions such as:

- 'What would the participants be doing now?' (At this point the activity may seem rather trainer-centred);
- 'What's the link between these two activities?' (The link may not be clear to participants. Quite often in *dry-runs* the need for transitions is seen);

- 'How does this fit in with the objectives?' (The course or you may be straying from the objectives).

At the end of the *dry-run*, collect the feedback sheets and some time later discuss specific comments and suggestions with participants privately. There is obviously a need for openness here, both from participants and yourself. Colleagues should give honest and direct feedback – tough enough to ensure that the necessary changes are made before the pilot presentation. In a similar constructive spirit, avoid being defensive about the course and your performance, listen to the criticisms and carefully consider any suggestions that are made.

You criticize the course

Your colleagues will have their views and suggestions, but they will not have worked and lived through the course development. Most important of all, you probably know your target population quite well now, whereas your colleagues do not. Based on your experience of conducting the session and input from colleagues, *you* need to criticize the course. You can adapt colleagues' suggestions and make them your own. But do not do things which are 'foreign' to you. If most of your experience is as a fairly orthodox trainer, do not be persuaded to change the course into a series of structured experiences. You might add some experiential activities like role-play or simulation, but if the course and the training style do not suit you, not only will you feel uncomfortable but participants will feel uncomfortable as well.

A good *dry-run* is particularly essential when time for course development is short. The dry-run will immediately provide the benefit of your colleagues' experience and expertise and give you the feel of the course in practice. A final product of this *dry-run* should be a list of points and material to be revised.

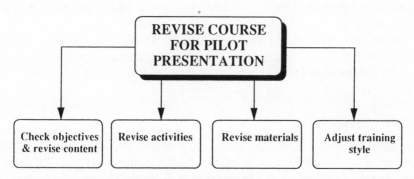

Product :   Trainer's Guide and Participant Handbook

Figure 3.12 *Revise course for pilot presentation*

Revise course for pilot presentation

Novice course developers are often surprised and sometimes upset by the number of revisions colleagues suggest. Instead they should be grateful.

Better to have a tough *dry-run* and a number of revisions than feel in the middle of your *pilot* presentation that everything is going wrong and getting out of control. Radical revisions are sometimes needed – there may be blood on the floor – but the final training is always better for it, and the pilot presentation can seem wonderfully easy compared to a difficult *dry-run*.

As a result of the *dry-run* and in preparation for the pilot you may need to take the following steps.

Check objectives and revise content

This usually results in a clarification or reduction in the number of objectives. Often the amount of information given directly to participants can be reduced in favour of more learning through the activities. The remaining content information can then be clarified or simplified, sometimes through the development of additional visual aids.

Revise activities

This usually entails clarifying the directions for activities and allocating them more time. Colleagues may suggest an additional activity or ways to prevent an activity getting 'bogged down'. For example, they may suggest reducing the 'stop points' during a videotape because you might get too involved in discussion. Other suggestions may relate to the form of an activity. Perhaps you could use small group work for this task? That would channel the expertise and energies of the more experienced participants and help the less experienced. Role-plays and simulations in particular can create time problems. As with discussions, participants can become greatly involved and if you have not allowed enough time you may have to rush the rest of the session. The *dry-run* should give an opportunity to test out role-plays and simulations, so that the final timing and agenda can be adjusted accordingly.

Revise materials

This again usually involves clarification eg, clearer overhead transparencies, the numbering of pages in the handbook, eliminating typing errors, etc. The *dry-run* often exposes many minor errors which, although trivial in themselves, can detract from the credibility of the course and the trainer.

Adjust training style

Colleagues may not comment on this but if some adjustment in training style is needed, you will probably recognize it in the *dry-run*. Changes in activities may help with the adjustment. For example, the introduction of group seating and more group activities will lead a rather authoritarian trainer towards a more 'facilitative' training style. Often the overall training style is set at the beginning of the course and revisions made to the introduction can establish a more directive or less directive role for the trainer. At times in the course you may need to be more directive, at other times less so; a situational training model can be helpful here (see Chapter 5).

The final product of this stage is a trainer's guide for the pilot presentation. This incorporates any changes and, as you write the guide, gives you one more chance to think through and fine-tune the training.

Project Action Items: Design a training course

1. Using the form below, prepare an action plan for a course you intend to design.

COMPLETION DATE	ACTION	RESPONSIBLE
	Initiate course design and development	
	Identify course objectives	
	Collect information and materials	
	Develop content, practice and application activities	
	Conduct a dry-run of the course	
	Revise course for pilot presentation	
	Conduct pilot presentation	
	Revise course materials for final printing	

2. Write performance objectives for this course. Remember to use action verbs.

_____

_____

_____

3. Meet with at least one other person to brainstorm some training methods. Make sure that you include a variety of methods and that they encourage participant involvement.List your methods

_____

_____

_____

4. Describe how you will evaluate participant performance.

_____

_____

_____

4

How to develop and use effective training materials

This chapter describes how to develop and use the most common training materials. The focus is on materials that you can produce and use with little or no professional help. Mostly we will discuss how to develop and use materials as part of, and to support direct or trainer-led training sessions. However, reference will also be made to how these materials can be adapted for 'self-managed' and 'open learning' situations.

'Chalk and talk' were at one time the main methods used by teachers and trainers to present new information. Over the past 20 years however, there has been a rapid increase in the variety and use of teaching and training aids. These range from print materials, flipcharts, overhead transparencies and slides that a single trainer can produce, to video, interactive video and computer-based training (CBT) where specialist assistance is necessary. You can use training aids to:

- Provide different kinds of information required for a course; for example, reading passages, case studies and role-play information.
- Increase the effectiveness of a course by attracting and holding the attention of participants.
- Reinforce the message. For example, you can use overhead transparencies as visual reinforcement for the points you make in a presentation. Similarly, a job aid reinforces the steps in a procedure.
- Promote increased participant involvement. You can do this through the use of attractive and interactive print and visual materials.
- Modify the attitudes and behaviour of participants. For example, participants' readiness to learn and change can be influenced by the use of questionnaires.
- Provide supplementary or reference material. You might use articles from magazines or passages from books as further reading for participants.

As well as providing support for group training sessions, training materials can also be used to cater for individual needs within a course. For example, one or

Figure 4.1 *Identify appropriate training materials*

more participants who need to work on a particular information or skills area might go to a team room, view a video and do some exercises. They then might rejoin the other participants for a discussion or brief presentation on what they have learned.

Increasingly materials are developed to provide individualized stand-alone training, for situations where the learner is working alone without any assistance from a trainer. This is self-managed or open learning where people organize their own programme and learn at a place, time and pace which suit their own needs and requirements. Self-managed or open learning generally involves video, film or slides together with print materials; trainer support may be provided on request or through regular meetings. Increasingly large companies are providing fully equipped learning centres where employees can use video, computers and reference resources to work on their own learning projects.

Identify appropriate training materials

One of the important questions you need to answer when developing a course is, 'What materials do I need to conduct this training and achieve the learning objectives?' There are, as we have seen, considerations of:

Content – what are the appropriate materials for this target population and their needs?
Delivery – what are the appropriate delivery methods for this group? How can I provide a variety of materials and media so that learning is enhanced?
Interest/motivation – what materials can I use to increase participant interest and motivation to learn?
Feasibility – what materials are most cost-effective and can most easily be used to conduct this training?

Find out what is already available

Just as in the development of a course, a first step in the development of materials is to find out what is already available. Review off-the-shelf materials, find out what is available and identify what is appropriate. You might be able to adapt or tailor off-the-shelf materials or those you have used for other courses to the requirements of a new course. For example, some of the transparencies and print materials you used for a course on supervisory skills might be used for a course on business meetings.

Decide what you can produce yourself

Consider here your own existing skills and any skills you might want to develop. For example, you may not have produced slides before but if a slide presentation is appropriate for the course, you might want to develop it yourself. Consider too, the resources available and how professional your materials should be for a particular training programme and target population.

Estimate costs in time and money

Estimate how much time it will take to produce any course materials. If you are using graphics or video professionals, you need to determine how much 'lead time' they will require and, once started, how long it will take them to produce the materials. You have a lot more control over your own time than other people's and you should try to avoid a situation where you are conducting a new course the next day for which the graphics or video are still not ready. Sometimes because of long 'lead times' it may be necessary to design and order visual aids on the basis of your course outline.

The question arises as to how professional, elaborate, or expensive materials should be. This depends on the audience and on how often the materials will be used. A group of top management people would have higher expectations in terms of professional visual and print materials than a group of on-the-job trainers. Other factors are the number of prospective participants and how many times the materials will be used. You might assess the materials cost per course and per participant. If the course will be taught many times and to a large number of participants, the cost of high quality materials becomes only a small part of the overall training cost. If however the cost per participant is high, management should be made aware of this.

Materials can of course have a multi-purpose quality when they are used for several courses. For example a video on how to make oral presentations might be used in a variety of training courses dealing with communication skills. It may also be used as part of an 'open learning package'. These multi-purpose possibilities are very important when considering the development of expensive materials such as video or computer-based training. Roughly speaking, the larger or more important the target population and the greater the interest taken by management, the more worthwhile it is to invest in the production of high-quality professional materials.

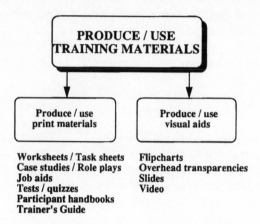

Figure 4.2 *Produce/use training materials*

In this section the focus is mainly on training materials that can be produced by a single teacher or trainer without much experience or expertise in materials production. First we shall look at the advantages and disadvantages of using particular materials in a training session, then consider how you might produce these training materials and use them in a training session.

Produce and use print materials

Of the various media that can be used to support training courses, print materials are the most versatile, reliable (there is no equipment to break down), most portable and least expensive. In this section we shall discuss:

- Worksheets/task sheets
- Job aids
- Quizzes or tests
- Participant handbooks
- Trainer's guides.

Worksheets/task sheets

- Reinforce the spoken word. For example, you might provide a presentation outline for participants to note down points or questions for use either in the discussion or for future reference. This avoids participants having to spend a lot of time copying down notes.
- Assess learning. For example, you can provide structured question sheets or worksheets where the answers that the learner enters are largely predetermined. These predictable responses can be included in the trainer's guide so that you can guide the discussion. Depending on the objectives and the topic, more 'open-ended' questions can also be asked. Here the responses are not so

predictable and the learner has scope for the expression of opinions or the creative application of knowledge or skills to his or her own situation. Often worksheets include several 'closed' questions asking for facts, together with an open-ended question at the end that pulls everything together and provides for a practical discussion.

■ Structure a group activity, case study, or role-play. Worksheets can be used to prepare participants for an activity and to reinforce the model they will use in the activity. For example the worksheet in Figure 4.3 was used to reinforce a coaching model and develop supervisors' coaching skills through a role play.

■ Structure observation and feedback on activities. A checklist or questionnaire can help either the trainer or selected participants to observe a group activity. The checklist or questionnaire enables the observer to focus on group interactions, skill performance and interpersonal skills and report on them later. The same checklist or questionnaire can also be used to help group members report, discuss and reflect on their activity.

When you develop a worksheet or task sheet:

■ Focus on the purposes of the worksheet and decide how best to achieve them. For example the worksheet in Figure 4.3 was designed to reinforce and give practice in using a coaching model.

■ Decide how the worksheet will be used. In particular, decide whether this activity should be individual, pair or group. You can make pair or group activities more challenging than individual activities where there is always a danger of embarrassing a participant. For example, in a questionnaire you might include more 'open' questions that involve the pair or group in some discussion before deciding on an answer.

■ Provide clear simple instructions giving the purpose of the worksheet and how to use it. Test out these instructions by having someone else read them for possible confusion or ambiguity.

■ Make any questions as short as possible. Use the active voice and short sentences.

■ Consider using a mix of rather general 'open' questions and 'closed' questions which ask for details. The open questions require participants to express their own ideas and opinions and encourage thought and discussion. The closed questions require participants to retrieve detailed information from a reading, film, video or other resource. Open questions tend to be most effective at the beginning or at the end of a worksheet. If you have an open question at the beginning, it can be used to lead into the topic and help you identify the individual participant's knowledge and attitudes. An open question at the end can be used for summary purposes, for a discussion about the applications of the course information, or simply to lead into a general discussion. Open questions can take up a lot of discussion time however, if they are in the middle of a worksheet, you might not reach the other questions.

■ Provide one or two questions which force participants to select relevant infor-

---

COACHING PREPARATION FORM

As a supervisor, you are going to coach one of your staff. Complete this form in preparation for the role-play.

Person to be coached: _____

Date: _____ Place: _____

Start and finish times: _____

Facts of the situation: _____

_____

_____

Objectives of the session – what you want to achieve:

_____

_____

1. State the problem exactly and clearly. Use descriptive statements:

_____

_____

2. Reach agreement that a problem exists. Questions to use/consequences if problem:

_____

_____

3. Discuss causes of the problem. Questions to use:

_____

_____

4. Discuss possible solutions and agree upon action(s). Identify specific action(s) to be taken.

_____

_____

5. Document the session. How?

_____

6. Follow-up on the session and recognize achievement of change. How? When? _____

_____

Figure 4.3 *Coaching worksheet*

mation and apply it to their job situations. For example, 'How can the speaker's ideas about motivating participants be used in your situation? Give at least three specific examples'. Note the wording of the question here. If the question was, 'Can the speaker's ideas about motivating participants be used in your situation?' then negative participants might get away with the short answer: 'They can't'. With the question worded as it is, participants are obliged to think about these ideas on motivation and try to apply them in their own situation. They are required to think of three specific examples and their answers should not only provide interesting reporting and discussion material, but important feedback on the progress of the course.

■ Try to limit your worksheet to one page. That will make it easier for participants to refer to and use.

■ Test out a worksheet several times before using it. Which instructions or questions are not clear? Which questions do participants need more space for answering? Do they need more explanation or guidance on a particular task?

■ Predict possible answers to your questions and plan how you will discuss participant responses. That way you can check on any confusion in the questions, avoid duplication (questions that lead to the same answers) and prepare yourself for a variety of responses.

Job aids

Technical manuals usually describe *all* the functions of a system. They often fail to focus on users' most common or urgent needs. Job aids which describe the most common or critical tasks can reduce the need for lengthy manuals and be used for a variety of purposes. They can:

■ Reduce the complexity of a task which involves many steps and where the consequences of error may be high.

■ Reduce the possibility of forgetting and are particularly useful for jobs performed infrequently.

■ Ensure a standard job performance and help the new or inexperienced employee to perform satisfactorily.

As a result job aids are now common in many occupations. Daily 'To Do' lists are kept by staff as *aides-mémoire* and to organize and make their day more productive. Pilots and astronauts use checklists particularly for pre-flight checks, and maintenance workers often use diagrams and decision tables when they are checking equipment. There is a variety of job aid formats:

■ Lists consisting of a set of steps to follow in sequence.

■ Checklists in which each item must be checked off when completed, for example an induction checklist that a supervisor might use to organize the induction of a new employee.

■ Forms where the information required is specified on the form.

■ Diagrams together with instructions, for example a diagram and instructions showing how to assemble a piece of equipment.

■ Worksheets where the calculations or data required are specified.

■ Decision tables with *if/then* rules for making decisions. These tables are used particularly in equipment maintenance and programming applications.

■ Flowcharts which indicate multiple decision paths and outcomes for each path. In flowcharts a rectangle usually represents an action and a diamond represents a decision.

■ Models which are examples or illustrations of what a procedure should look like, for example the six-step coaching model shown in Figure 4.3.

When they are used in training situations job aids can:

■ Force the client and the subject specialists to define what they see as the desired performance. The training objectives are therefore made a lot clearer.
■ Save the memorization of a procedure learnt in a course. The job aid can be included in the participant handbook so that participants can refer to it later and perhaps make multiple copies for use on the job.
■ Save money as job aids may be used as an alternative to formal training or as a means of reducing training time. In the first flood of enthusiasm for job aids, the need for training was often neglected. Increasingly however training courses are built around when and how to use a job aid. Simulations,which may involve videotaped performances of the job, may be used to give participants practice in using the aid.

There are however some problems in using job aids:

■ It is sometimes difficult to get them used on the actual job. They need to be practical, easy to use and integrated into job activities. When introducing a job aid you need to convince participants it will actually help them. You also need to provide guidelines that participants can follow and practise in using the aid. For example in time management courses, trainers generally recommend that *To Do* lists should be completed at the end of the day or at the beginning of the next day. Practice in filling in a *To Do* list is also often provided during the course.
■ Experienced participants do not need as much detail as new participants. If you make the job aid highly detailed, experienced participants will not use it. Yet if it is not detailed enough, it will provide insufficient help to new staff.
■ Job aids do not develop an understanding of the principles or theory of an operation. An understanding of principles or theory enables someone to trouble-shoot and generate solutions for a new situation or application. Training therefore needs to be given together with job aid practice in order to provide the principles or theory and a variety of applications.

Here are some tips for developing job aids:

■ Make sure the job aid is task-specific. It may become confusing and hard to use if it lists all available functions.
■ Keep the steps of a procedure in the sequence that they need to be done.
■ Include only necessary steps in the procedure. Avoid including 'nice to know' or other supplemental information.
■ Use clear simple language – short sentence and the active voice.
■ With complicated processes or tasks, show the consequences of each step so that users can be sure that they have completed each one correctly.

■ Design job aids so that they can be posted in locations easily accessible to the user.
■ Use colour to make critical job aids or critical steps stand out.

Quizzes or tests

Beginning a training session with a simple true/false or multiple choice quiz can be an effective way to get participants' attention and involvement. It can also help participants recognize the value of the training, provide an outline of what is to be covered and help you assess the level of knowledge and experience in the group. For example, near the beginning of a company induction you might give a light-hearted quiz asking questions about the company, its history, number of employees, area where it's located, main products, etc. In this way you would find out what participants already know about the company and its context.

Quizzes or short tests can also be used in the middle of a course. For example in a multiple-day course, as part of your review of the previous day's information you might give a short quiz.

At the end of a training course also you might have a review or post-test. For example, at the beginning of a course you might give a quiz to assess participants' current knowledge and to indicate the subject areas to be covered. Then at the end of the course you might give the same quiz again. The difference in scores would indicate to yourself and participants how much of the course information had been assimilated. Another way to handle a review quiz is to ask the participants themselves to prepare the test with so many test items from each pair or group. You can then collect these items, check them and standardize the format before giving the test. In this way you can reinforce and assess the information participants have gained from the course. (For more information on quizzes, see Chapter 6.)

Participant handbooks

Participant handbooks can be used as a guide and reference through a course. They can also be used after the training as a reference source.

When you are developing the course decide what print materials should go into the participant handbook and what will be more effective as single handouts. For example, tests, quizzes or questionnaires may be more effective as single handouts because there is always a danger of participants reading ahead and completing these tasks before you want them to. Here is a list of materials that you might consider including in your participant handbook:

■ A page giving the title, objectives and agenda for the course.
■ Section dividers for each module of course material.
■ Pre-course reading material or tasks with questions. Participants sometimes forget to bring the pre-course reading material or tasks with them.
■ In-course reading materials, for example reprints of articles on course topics.

- Worksheets or task sheets, for example the questions on a videotape.
- Case studies – all the material required for the case study can be included in the handbook.
- Group tasks – the instructions for the task need to be included and the remainder of the page can be used by participants to make notes on the task or to prepare their group report.
- Role play materials.
- Copies of those overhead transparencies or slides that participants might want to make notes on or refer to later. This saves them trying to quickly copy down information from the visual aids.
- Schematics or flowcharts of any technical processes described in the course.
- Graphs or charts that are referred to in the course.
- Job aids that participants can actually use at work eg, checklists.
- Action plan page or pages for a learning log.
- A list of resources or references. This might be included when a large number of sources have been used in the course development and participants may want to check these sources or read further.

Trainer's guide

A trainer's guide may simply be a guide for yourself and as basic as a participant handbook with annotations. The guide however must be more detailed if someone else is to use it. In particular, it can prove valuable when a trainer new to the topic has to conduct the course, the course needs to be presented again after a long time, or the course has to be revised. Here is a list of what might be included in a trainer's guide.

- Course description, objectives and other information such as target population for the course and any prerequisites.
- Training outline including what the trainer presents and details of how the activities (group task, discussion, etc.) might be handled. Each page in the trainer's guide should face a copy of the relevant page in the participant handbook.
- Print copies of the transparencies and slides used in the course.
- Optional activities. This should not be a ragbag of activities but a few exercises that a trainer might use in order to adjust the course to a specific group of participants or to fit his or her own training style and interests.
- Copies of relevant articles, for example pre-reading or follow-up material.
- List of resources used – books and articles, titles of films or videos, etc. Another trainer might need to consult these resources, particularly if revising the course.
- Transparency, slide and handout masters for possible duplication.

Produce and use visual aids

Studies have shown that speakers using visual aids are perceived as being better prepared, more professional, clearer, more interesting and more concise when compared to speakers who do not use visuals. Visual aids however are not a simple recipe for success. They need to be appropriate, well-produced and used effectively. Here are a few general points about their use. Visual aids should:

■ Enhance a presentation, not compete with it. In other words, you should not allow visuals to distract attention from the information being presented.

■ Present information concisely and clarify relationships between points, parts of something or the stages in a process. In particular, visual aids such as transparencies and slides can be used to provide an overview or summary of the course information and activities.

■ Supplement and support the course information and activities. Visual aids can reinforce and promote communication by focusing on key words and concepts, thus reducing the risk of misunderstanding.

■ Provide a concrete reference and show things that are normally inaccessible. For example, equipment that is too large or too difficult to bring into the training room or workshop can be represented by a visual aid.

As we saw in Chapter 1, visual aids greatly increase retention and learning. They do this not only because of their appeal to the eye, but because they generate more interest and offer a change of pace. They capture the participants' attention.

Here are some guidelines and suggestions for developing and using the most common visual aids:

■ Flipcharts
■ Overhead transparencies
■ Slides
■ Commercial video and film
■ In-house video.

Flipcharts

The blackboard always evokes memories of school. The flipchart however is identified with business and industry and reinforces an adult meeting atmosphere. Flipcharts are particularly effective with small audiences because they have an informal appearance that encourages discussion between the audience and the speaker.

Another advantage of the flipchart is flexibility. Prepared pages or a prepared flipchart can be brought to the session. The advantages of these prepared pages are that you can:

■ Produce them in neat and legible writing.

- Save time in the training session or presentation by not having to write up these pages.
- Use the pages as guidelines or notes for yourself.

A prepared flipchart or prepared pages can be used in conjunction with 'ad lib' pages or an 'ad lib' flipchart that you produce during the session. The prepared pages might be used to show the title of the training session or presentation, the objectives, the agenda, instructions for a specific task, models, steps, or other material that you know you will use. Obviously these prepared pages can be used again in later training sessions or presentations.

The 'ad lib' pages or flipchart can be used to record responses that you obtain from people, group work reports, or other feedback information. Compared to alternative media, the flipchart is easily portable and you can roll up your prepared flipcharts and use them away from your usual work site.

Preparing the flipchart

- Decide what pages you want to prepare in advance and which pages you will produce as a result of discussion or group activities. Draft your prepared pages on sheets of paper or cards before you actually begin work on the flipchart.
- Lay the flipchart on a flat surface so that you can work easily with it. If possible, use water colour markers – permanent markers often bleed through onto the next page.
- On each page write down only the main points and limit these to no more than five or six. Abbreviate any long words or sentences. You can explain and add more detail when you refer to these points in your training session.
- Leave a blank page between each page you write. Flipchart pages tend to be thin and can be read through. When you are referring to one page you don't want your audience to be reading the next one.
- Give each page a printed heading and write clearly with letters at least two inches high. Most people's writing tends to be too small. Leave about one and a half inches between key points. Lightly squared flipchart pages can help with spacing but if these are unavailable, use a ruler and pencil to make guidelines. Then, after you've written down your information, erase the guidelines.
- Use two or three colours for variety and to emphasize key points or key words. The page heading should be a different colour from the points. Avoid pale colours such as yellow and pastels – they are hard to see from a distance.
- If you expect to refer to a flipchart page more than once, mark it with a paper clip or a sticker.
- Fix the flipchart on a flipchart stand. Check the stand for stability and go through the pages as you will during the training session. Check that the pages are in the correct sequence and that there is nothing more you need to add.
- If you are travelling with prepared flipchart pages, tear them off the pad, roll them up and place them in a cardboard tube.

Using the flipchart

During your presentation you can produce 'ad lib' pages as a result of the information obtained from participants, the discussions or group activities. When you use the flipchart:

■ Stand at the side as you speak and write so that you can maintain eye contact with participants. Avoid talking to the board as you write things down.
■ Make sure your audience can see what you write. Don't use small writing or small diagrams.
■ Make sure each new page has a printed heading. This improves the appearance of your pages and makes it easier to review later.
■ Record only the main ideas. Limit the number of points on a page to no more than five or six and do not fill a page to the bottom. People at the back of the room may not be able to see.
■ Use a pointer to indicate important ideas, then turn to the audience and speak.
■ Pause after you complete a page. Before you turn to a new page, allow time for participants to read and if necessary make notes.
■ Let participants use flipchart pages to record the results of their group work. This makes it easier for the results to be discussed afterwards.
■ Tear off pages and tape them up on the wall for easy reference later in the session.
■ Turn to a blank sheet or the cover page when you finish. Flipchart pages showing from a previous activity can distract people from a new activity.

Overhead transparencies

Overhead transparencies (OHTs) are more formal than the flipchart and work well with audiences of small to moderate size. When you use OHTs this helps your planning and leads to more organized and effective training sessions. You seem better prepared, more professional, more persuasive and more in control. There is a tendency therefore for audiences to accept your ideas or plans and for favourable decisions to be reached.

Preparing your OHTs early helps you with your outlining and to focus on the main points. The main content of your training session appears on the OHTs and you can use them over and over again and ensure a consistent presentation.

Developing overhead transparencies

■ When you prepare an outline for your training session indicate important points where you might use OHTs.
■ Draft your OHTs on sheets of paper or cards. For each transparency decide what the message is and what the key ideas and words are.
■ Check whether you can replace a 'words-only' transparency with a graphic or add a relevant picture or diagram to add interest to the text. Remember transparencies are *visual aids* and the more variety you can add, the better the participants' response.

■ If you are using words, follow the six by six rule. Try to express your *one idea or message* in a maximum of six lines with no more than six words a line. More information and words than this can lead to confusion and the loss of the central message. In particular, you should avoid treating OHTs like pages in a book and filling the screen with information and small print.

■ Use key words and phrases rather than sentences. Then you can expand on these points in your presentation, rather than just read the text being projected. When you use key words and phrases however, preserve grammatical parallelism. The points should all begin with the same part of speech – action verbs or nouns, etc.

■ Choose a clear and consistent design for your transparencies and concentrate information in the centre. Most screens are horizontal so use a horizontal format to allow full use of the screen and make it easier to project over the heads of participants. Avoid vertical lettering on your OHTs as it is difficult to read.

■ Leave a three-quarter inch margin for the frame. Letters should be at least one inch high for good legibility with half an inch between lines. Rule lines in pencil to keep your letters the same size and on a line, then erase the pencil lines afterwards.

■ Direct attention to the key ideas by using colour, boxing or underlining. Be consistent and use the same colours for headings, numbering, etc.

■ Use tinted transparency film if you want to colour code your transparencies. You might use the same tint for a series of OHTs on one topic, then change the background tint for another topic.

■ Use bullets (•) or check marks (✓) rather than numbers when you are listing items that are not sequential eg, the features of a project.

■ Do not reproduce a printed page on a transparency. The diagram or writing will be too small.

■ Use overlays – one or more additional transparencies placed on top of the original one – when you want to show the stages in a project or process. Each additional transparency builds upon the previous ones until the entire visual process is complete. Taping overlays to a cardboard frame can ensure sharp alignment of transparencies during a training session or presentation.

Transparency production

If you do not have graphics professionals or access to computer graphics, you can produce your own OHTs as follows:

■ Produce the graphic on A4 paper. A piece of graph paper under the transparency film can be used as a lettering guide.

■ Alternatively you might use a lettering system. You can colour the letters in later with permanent overhead projector pens. Use colour as much as possible and whatever you do, avoid typing on transparencies. Type is much too small for people to read and makes your transparencies look dull and amateur.

■ Photocopy the graphic onto transparency film with a normal copier, or use a thermofax copier.

■ Mount the OHTs in cardboard frames. These frames make useful places to put your notes – either on the frame itself or on a sticker – and can help guide you through the presentation. Notes will be particularly useful if this is the first time you have made the presentation. Frames also make transparencies easier to transport and store.

Preparing transparencies

■ Number your OHTs on the frames so that if they are knocked on the floor or mixed up, you can sort them out. If you are undecided on the order or may change it, number the transparencies in pencil or use easily removed labels.

■ Analyse your OHTs and see if any can be eliminated. Some transparencies might be optional – eliminated if it's necessary to shorten the session, or included if it's necessary to give further explanation or lengthen the session. Dealing with transparencies in this way gives you more flexibility in your training session.

■ Practice using the transparencies before the course and try to ensure a smooth link between your narrative and your OHTs.

■ Make sure the projector lens and the projection surface are clean before you start.

■ To ensure that your transparencies don't project crookedly, tape a straight-edged piece of cardboard along the top edge of the projector surface. Then slide each new transparency against the straight edge.

■ Make sure your projector works well and a spare projector or bulb is available. When you're setting up the room for your course, use your first transparency, walk to the back of the room and view the transparency as a course participant – check it for clarity, screen placement and image distortion.

Using overhead transparencies

■ Provide participants with print copies of your transparencies. This gives them a reference or record and prevents interruptions when people who want to make notes ask you to keep a transparency on the screen. If participants don't have to copy your points, they can focus on listening to you and understanding the information.

■ Use the projector with the room lights on. You might dim the lights but don't distract people by constantly switching them on and off.

■ As much as possible, maintain eye contact with participants. Stand at the side of the projector and read any points from the transparency, rather than the screen. If you read from or talk to the screen, participants will see only your back and you will miss any facial expressions or body language that indicate confusion or disagreement.

■ Avoid getting between the overhead projector and the screen or blocking the participants' view.

■ Mask information. Control the pace and give a sense of movement to your presentation by masking parts of transparencies with a piece of card or paper. The masking card or piece of paper should be placed *beneath* the transparency and then slid down – if you put the mask on top of the transparency, you will need to hold it there to prevent it dropping off. Use the mask to gradually reveal each point as you deal with it so that the visual and verbal focus is on one point at a time. This is particularly important when you have lists of points. If your audience can see all the points, they may be reading point 6 when you are talking about point 1. Participants may also spend time copying things down and miss your comments. Through masking you can avoid this and link the transparency directly with your narrative.

■ Do not use so many OHTs that the projector becomes a reading machine. Overhead transparencies are a *visual* medium.

■ Use a pointer and point at the transparency, *not at the screen*. Pointing at the screen casts shadows and takes you away from the audience. You can leave the pointer or pen on the transparency pointing to something while you talk about it.

■ Do not flip transparencies on and off. Give participants time to absorb the material and make any notes.

■ Use the on/off switch effectively. When you want the audience to focus on a transparency, switch on. When you want them to focus on you and what you are saying, switch off. In particular, do not leave the projector switched on for a long time without a transparency in place. This distracts attention from what you are saying or doing.

■ Increase group involvement. Elicit information or ideas from participants and use water-soluble transparency markers to write them on a blank transparency.

Slides

Slides tend to be more formal and authoritative than the flipchart or OHTs and are often used for business or project briefings to management audiences. Slides generally discourage discussion and participant interaction because of their formal appearance and because the lighting is dimmed. After the slide presentation is over however, you might turn up the lights and generate a discussion or group activity.

Preparing slides

■ Complete a small index card for each slide. Describe what appears on the slide and indicate any production notes, such as whether the slide should be a long shot or close up. Below this or on the other side of the card write down what you plan to say when you present the slide. After completing all the cards, put them into sequence. You can move, add, or delete cards to complete your presentation. Once they are numbered, the cards become your shooting script.

■ Use photographs, diagrams, charts, graphs, or flowcharts. A slide presentation needs to be visual and there should be a variety of images. If you have only words to show, you might add computer clip-art figures or insert photographs to highlight the main idea.

■ Vary the pace of your presentation. Provide some slides – for example, charts and graphs – which you will spend time on and discuss. These can be supported by photographs or illustrations which you might move through quickly.

■ Use the six by six rule and condense any verbal information on the slides into not more than six lines and six words per line. Keep the words on the slides horizontal, especially on charts.

■ When one slide remains on the screen for too long, people's minds begin to wander. A long-winded speaker showing five or six points on slide may lose the audience. When you show a new slide however, it's like poking the audience in the side and you regain their attention. Just as the OHT revelation technique highlights new points and retains audience attention, the *progressive disclosure* or *build* technique can be used with slides. Here is how it works. If you want to make four points, highlight each new point with a new slide. The first slide contains the title and the first point. The second slide has the title and two points with the new point highlighted and the first point in a darker colour or shaded. The third slide has the third point highlighted and the earlier two points de-emphasized. This continues for the remaining point or points. The same technique can be applied to slides which show charts. A line at a time can be added to show trends in a line chart. One or two bars at a time can be added to a bar chart to dramatize change or growth.

■ Use a consistent design for your series of slides and follow the same design rules as for overhead transparencies. You might use several colours in your diagrams or charts but for the background it's best to use just one colour.

Using slides

The following points will help you when you use slides. Before you start:

■ Check the focus and picture size on the screen. The greater the distance between the projector and the screen, the larger the picture. To determine maximum viewing distance, use eight times the height of the projected image.

■ Rehearse to check that each slide in the carousel is in the correct sequence and the right way up. Each slide should have a number on a sticker in the top right hand corner.

When you start:

■ Introduce the slide programme. You might make the session more interactive by inviting the audience to look at particular items for discussion afterwards.

■ Sound interested and enthusiastic to overcome any passive TV-watching atmosphere.

■ Use the remote control and stand well away from the projector, facing the audience.

■ Expand upon what is on the screen but don't read too much text from the slides. Reading from slides is irritating when people can read themselves.

■ Be prepared to move back to particular slides during the question and answer session.

Commercial video and film

Every year *Training* magazine conducts a survey of training and development in US companies; since 1987 video has been the most popular medium in company training. Major reasons for video's popularity are its convenience and ease of use. Compared with film, video is easier to stop and start and therefore comment on; it also tends to be easier to use than film and more hardy. Another factor in this growing popularity has been the rapid increase in the number of videos produced for training and development purposes.

Showing a video by itself however is not training. You need to pay attention to selecting an appropriate video – one which fits your objectives and your participants and can be integrated with other activities in your training session.

Selecting video

The video assessment report, Figure 4.4, can be used in order to select videos. The following notes explain how the report might be used.

Purpose(s) of assessment – you might note the particular reasons why you are reviewing this video.

Video title – write down the title.

Running time – more than 20 minutes without a stop or pause point usually bores people. You also need the timing for your agenda or session plan.

Cost – note the rental and purchase costs. Will you use this video enough times to justify purchase?

Session topic – identify the topic of your training session.

Session objective(s) – writing your objectives down will help you to focus on how closely the video fits them.

Useful training points – here you might note the main ideas covered in the video or points you might focus on in the activity following the programme.

Advantages of using this video – listing these will support any justification required and help you make up your own mind as to the value of using the programme.

Disadvantages of using this video – identify any problems or confusions that might arise.

How to overcome disadvantages – how might you introduce the video to prevent problems or confusion arising? Perhaps you could stop or pause the video at any difficult or potentially confusing points and then explain.

Cost justification (based on number of participants or importance of training) – programme cost per participant is a good measure, but you also need to consider

Video assessment report

Purpose(s) of assessment: _____

_____

Video title: _____

Running time: _____ Cost: _____

Session topic: _____

_____

Session objective(s):_____

_____

_____

VIDEO FEATURES		
	YES	**NO**
Fits in with session objective(s)		
Fits employees' knowledge and skills levels		
Gains and maintains employee interest		
Provides appropriate content and examples		
Uses appropriate language with minimal jargon		
Provides up-to-date information		
Is segmented with stop or pause points		
Is supported by a trainer guide		
Is supported by exercises or actitivies		
Is satisfactory in terms of technical quality		
Fits the type of playback equipment available		

Useful training points: _____

_____

_____

Advantages of using this video: _____

_____

Disadvantages of using this video: _____

_____

How to overcome disadvantages: _____

_____

Cost justification (based on number of participants or importance of training):

_____

Figure 4.4 *Video assessment report*

other factors such as the number of times the course may be conducted and the relative importance of the training programme.

Now use the Video Features checklist to assess the potential effectiveness of the video.

Fits in with session objective(s) – video purely for the sake of variety is a mistake. A video may be very interesting but if it doesn't support your objectives, it can distract participants from the message you're trying to convey.

Fits employees' knowledge and skill levels – a video that seems basic will 'turn off' participants. Conversely, a video which assumes a slightly higher knowledge or skill level than the participants possess may flatter them and often prove successful.

Gains and maintains employee interest – the first few minutes of the video are critical. Participants need to listen actively, not just watch TV.

Provides appropriate content and examples – check that the programme presents characters and situations which your participants can relate to. A group of professionals are not likely to be impressed if the characters in a video are clerical staff. A group of British salesmen are not likely to be influenced if the video characters are women working in the US.

Uses appropriate language with minimal jargon – put yourself in the place of your audience. Is there too much jargon for them? Does the video speak down to them or could it be considered infantile? American programmes often use cartoon characters but British participants tend to react with hostility to the cartoon approach.

Provides up-to-date information – if the programme seems old-fashioned and out-of-date, this tends to make you and your training seem old-fashioned and out-of-date.

Is segmented with stop or pause points – these points will enable you to make the session more interactive and give you more control over the training material.

Is supported by a trainer guide – a guide saves time and often provides some useful suggestions for activities.

Is supported by exercises or activities – again this will save you development time. Even if you don't use these materials as they stand, you might adapt them for your own specific purposes.

Is satisfactory in terms of technical quality – even minor faults can result in major distractions. Don't risk using a poor quality programme.

Fits the type of playback equipment available – you need to check that you have the necessary playback equipment available. There are a variety of video standards with NTSC being the US standard and PAL/SECAM being the standard in Britain and Europe. These formats and standards are not interchangeable so you need to check that the video is compatible with your equipment.

Additional points or features you want to consider might be added in the checklist blanks.

Preparing to show video

■ Once you have selected a video, preview it once more to become familiar with the parts you plan to use. Make notes while you watch so that you can explain complex topics and develop support materials. Note-making will make you familiar enough with the video to discuss it with participants and also help you prepare oral or written questions to guide a discussion.

■ If you intend to use only part of a video or stop at certain points, make a note of the counter numbers where you plan to stop and restart the programme.

■ Plan activities to accompany the video. These may range from informal discussion, a questionnaire on the programme content, or application exercises in which participants use what they have learned.

■ Prepare handouts to support the programme: for example, one handout might restate critical points in the video while another provides a series of questions.

■ Make sure that you know how to use the video equipment and that it works properly. Check the connections and controls are adjusted properly. Rehearse so that you can present the programme and the accompanying activities smoothly.

Using video

When you use video in your training session or presentation you might follow this sequence:

■ Prevent potential interruptions by disconnecting any phones and closing the door to the room.

■ Introduce the video and tell participants what they might pay attention to.

■ Tell them about the discussion or activities that follow the video. This will help participants focus on what they might learn from the programme. You might also challenge them with a question to be answered at the end of the video. This should be a question that is relevant to the objectives and personally interesting – one which obliges participants to apply the information from the video to their own personal or job situation. Alternatively, you might give participants a question sheet covering important information they should look for in the programme.

■ Darken the room enough for the video to be seen clearly, but leave some lights on so that participants can make notes.

■ Stay in the room while the video is on and model the attentive behaviour you expect of participants. Don't let them think the video is being shown just for you to have a break. Observe participants' reactions to the programme – this will help you decide how to approach the follow-up session.

■ Stop the video at intervals to discuss major steps in a particular process, the meaning of concepts, or specific situations. These stop-go techniques engage participants' attention, prevent them getting overloaded with information and transform a one-way communication experience into an active one. But don't stop the programme for too long or too often. You might destroy the continuity of the programme or detract from the interest and value of the follow-up activity. You might also find yourself short of time.

■ After the video you might:
  - repeat the question(s) you asked before the programme. These could lead into the follow-up task or discussion;
  - ask participants to work individually or in pairs to complete a questionnaire;
  - ask participants to work on an application task. This may involve them dividing into groups and finding ways to apply the video information to their own situations;
  - lead a discussion. First you might reinforce or elicit some of the key points made in the video, then ask how participants' experience relates to the programme and situations illustrated. Through the discussion you can integrate the purpose and content of the video with the rest of the training session.

In-house video

Since the 1970s companies have been producing their own videos for purposes of employee information, induction of new staff and training. Since 1988, the budgets that US companies have earmarked for producing training videos have increased by 42 per cent (*Training*, September 1993). Videos developed by the training departments of large companies have become increasingly sophisticated.

This section however will focus on the trainer's role in using video and the production of what might be called basic training videos. This includes:

■ Video recording of participants' performance in a training session. The recording can be done by the trainer or participants and is used for feedback purposes.
■ Video production. To support course training objectives a trainer can produce or be involved in producing video of job situations. For example you may want to show examples of team meetings, demonstrations of how to do a task, how particular processes work, or a whole variety of work situations.

Video recording

Video is a good teacher when you are training people in presentation, demonstration, or in interpersonal skills like how to conduct a meeting or lead a project team. Video is also a versatile training tool and the new light compact camcorders make it possible to tape easily in the classroom or at the work-site.

Using video to record participant presentations or activities during a course has the following advantages:

■ Participants see themselves in action and as others see them. The view that 'Others (the trainer or participants) are telling me what I'm like' becomes, 'This is what I'm like'. The experience gives participants a fresh perspective and increased control over their behaviour. In particular, video feedback builds up participants' self-confidence by highlighting strengths and indicating the specific areas where they can improve.

■ The assessment of participants' performance and the evaluation of skill levels are made more objective. Video provides tangible support and concrete examples for the trainer's assessment and suggestions for improvement.

■ During a training course, simulations or role-play situations such as job interviews or meetings can be evaluated by the participants and provide material for discussion.

■ Video stores information which can be retrieved. Participants can be given an opportunity to look at their performance privately after the course. The tape may also be used as a reference for a follow-up meeting at the job site.

Use

Do the recording yourself rather than rely on technical assistance. Keep the equipment under your own control and aim to produce a successful training activity rather than a dramatic film.

Filming from a fixed position without moving the camera is usually perfectly adequate for training purposes. Indeed it is often unnecessary or undesirable to zoom in and zoom out. The purpose is to get a straightforward and undistracting record of the meeting, presentation, etc.

When you are videotaping participants, defuse any nervousness by mentioning at the beginning of the recording that the tapes will be erased and nothing will be shown to participants' supervisors.

View participant demonstrations or presentations privately. If the viewing is done in public with other participants watching, the 'performer' may feel threatened by any suggestions and respond defensively. People also tend to be more critical of a person's performance as shown on videotape than they are of the actual performance.

Be sensitive and sympathetic in giving either public or private feedback. You might use questions and statements such as:

'Have you seen yourself on video before? It was quite a shock when *I* first saw myself'.
'Are there any things you think we should look at particularly?'.
'Let's look through the comments on people's feedback forms'.
'How do you think the demonstration/presentation could have been improved?'.

Try to relax participants and overcome any defensiveness or lack of confidence with some positive comments. People do not argue with their own data – whether these come from a self-assessment questionnaire they complete or a videotape recording. Therefore you might let the participant watch and comment on his or her performance and pause and stop the tape where necessary.

If the participant is confident because he or she did a good job, you might confirm that and then say, 'Let's look for ways in which it could have been even better'. Both of you might discuss how the performance might be improved in future.

Video production

It is always cheaper to buy video than to produce it yourself. Before you think of developing a video you need to find out if there is already something suitable for your needs and your target population (see References and Further Resources for a list of video providers). You can use an evaluation form like Figure 4.4. to review what is available.

---

1. What training objectives will this video project achieve? List them.

   _____

   _____

2. Describe your audience – number of people, jobs, work locations, training needs, levels of education and experience.

   _____

   _____

3. How familiar are the audience with the video content? What do they know already about the subject matter?

   _____

   _____

4. What benefits might the audience gain from the video? How will the video help them in their work?

   _____

   _____

5. What style and approach would best suit this audience? How should the training information be presented?

   _____

6. List some potential problems in developing this video.

   _____

7. What are some alternatives, solutions and means for overcoming the problems listed above?

   _____

   _____

Figure 4.5 *Video planner*

If you cannot find anything appropriate and decide that a video will help you achieve your training objectives, discuss your ideas with a video specialist. A form like the video planner, Figure 4.5, can be used to plan a production and force you and the video producer to respond to critical planning questions. In particular it can help you both to identify potential problems. For example, can written approvals for the 'shooting' locations be obtained easily? If you plan to use specific personnel, will they be available on the days you will be taping? Will this require written permission from their managers? The producer needs to check whether the necessary equipment is available, is there a need for additional equipment to be rented or bought? Once these potential problems are identified you can work with the producer to find some alternatives, solutions and means for overcoming them. Perhaps you can reduce the number of shooting locations, use staff in your own department as actors, or justify new equipment by reference to other video projects your management may be interested in.

Development guidelines

Editing video is very expensive and every hour of preparation at the beginning of a project can save many hours of editing at the end. When you are developing a video therefore you need to plan and schedule everything in advance. The trainer's involvement in developing video is mainly at the initial stages: in planning and developing the script. Here are some suggestions:

■ Discuss your project with others who produce training videos. The more input you can get on your project's feasibility and your plans, the better.
■ Explain to everyone involved the scope, purpose and importance of the whole project – how the video is part of or supports the training. These explanations about the training purposes will encourage the producer and his or her crew to look at their efforts in terms of instructional impact.
■ Encourage the producer to contribute ideas on the script; he or she knows what will work and will not work on the screen. Treat the producer as a creative collaborator, not just a technician who's going to put your great thoughts on video.
■ Keep the video short and simple. The exact length depends on the nature and scope of the instructional material but 15 to 20 minutes is usually sufficient for a training video.
■ Work with the producer to develop a script or *storyboard* outlining the visual and audio content of your video. In this way you can visualize each shot as it corresponds with the narration. Determine long shots, medium shots, close-ups, graphics, etc. and include this information on the storyboard.
■ Work with the producer to estimate the cost of the project. Important cost factors include the number of outside locations required (studio shooting takes less time and costs less), the cost of the studio, the expenses of any 'talent' (narrator/actors) you will need, the number and sophistication of graphics and the amount of editing required. In terms of cost there are two alternatives. The first is to start with a set budget and script accordingly. The other is to write

the script and then estimate the costs. In this case until you've produced the script, neither you nor the producer know how long the project will take, what materials you will require and what might be the final cost.

■ Working with the producer, select a presentation mode or combination of modes- demonstration, dramatization, interview.

■ Develop graphics – simple charts, graphs, or diagrams – to emphasize points or to summarize information. The same rules apply to the design of video graphics as for the design of transparencies or slides.

■ Be creative. Imaginative design, graphics and editing, good writing and re-search are the keys to quality, not sophisticated equipment and big budgets. Quite often you can find ways to reduce costs which also improve the effec-tiveness of your training video.

■ Before you start any video production, make certain that clients and your own management fully comprehend the demands, costs, benefits and limitations of the video project. In particular, you should always use a client-approved script to avoid arguments and expensive changes later.

■ Proofread your script some time before the 'shoot' so that you can still make improvements. Remember the KISS principle: any changes in language should simplify rather than complicate the message and if a sentence is hard to read, break it up into two sentences.

■ Throughout the production process, be receptive to changes, new ideas and suggestions. Flexibility and openness to change will add freshness to your project.

Production guidelines

The producer is responsible for putting your instructional message on video and the activities listed below are mainly his or her responsibility. It helps you work together more effectively however if you know something about the producer's work and concerns. The producer should:

■ Develop a production schedule specifying times and locations for rehearsals and shooting. Coordination is required with everyone – the client, video crew, people at the location, actors, etc. – so the producer needs to spend a lot of time on scheduling and follow-up.

■ Identify locations for the 'shoot' and make sure that the necessary permissions are obtained ahead of time. You and the producer may need to work together to reduce the number of locations – this not only saves time and money but can reduce potential confusion among viewers.

■ Get to know the locations for the 'shoot'. Both you and the producer should pay an advance visit to meet people, look at camera angles and check on technical matters such as whether the electrical system can handle the load from the lights, etc. This visit should also help you decide when to shoot. Video shot outside is best shot in the early morning or the last hour of the day – Steven Spielberg's 'golden hour'. Choose a time when there is the least chance of interruptions, distracting noises, etc. Finally, make sure that the people at the location know what is going to happen, when it is going to happen and how they'll be involved. Get them on your side.

■ Check to make sure you have everything needed before you leave for shooting. It is not only frustrating but very expensive if a piece of equipment is forgotten, or something isn't working and there is no back-up.

■ Closely monitor picture and audio levels during taping, paying close attention to picture composition. The producer needs to log shots and reduce the possibility of editing problems by overshooting. The same things should be shot from different angles and if the producer or you are not satisfied with a scene, it's best to shoot it again. Do not wait until you see the scene later in the editing suite; returning to the location and setting up the scene again is very expensive.

■ Shoot more than enough cutaways eg, an interviewer shaking his or her head, an apprentice watching a demonstration. The producer will need this footage later to help cover disorienting jump shots and poor edits.

■ Get everyone who appears or speaks on the tape to sign release forms granting you permission to produce and distribute the video.

■ Label every tape. Whether shooting on location or in a studio the producer needs to keep track of tapes and label them correctly. This is the best way to ensure against time-consuming mix ups.

■ Always make a copy of the completed master tape. Loss, theft, accidents or editing mistakes can happen and destroy the product of all your hard work.

Working on a video production can be a stimulating experience for a trainer and contribute to an effective training course. Video production however is a team effort. You need to be prepared to spend time working closely with the producer and technical crew to ensure that your instructional message 'gets across'.

Assess and revise materials

The assessment and revision of materials is part of the overall assessment and revision of a training course. As mentioned in Chapter 3, you should use feedback

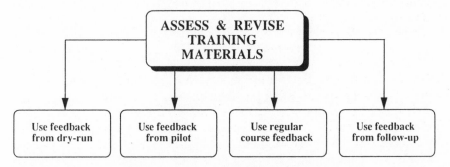

Figure 4.6 *Assess and revise training materials*

from the *dry-run* presentation of the course. Most of the materials revision tends to be done then. After the pilot, the first public presentation of your course, you should assess the materials and revise accordingly. Regular course feedback and feedback from follow-up observations may lead to additional revisions, but this is generally more fine-tuning.

Project Action Items: Develop training materials for your course

1. Develop an overhead transparency, slide or flipchart page which provides an outline of your course and lists the main points or sections. Make sure you follow the guidelines on visual aids given in this chapter.

2. Design at least five visual aids for your course. If your overview transparency or slide lists five main points, you should design a transparency, slide, or flipchart page for each of these points. Try to avoid an 'all word' series. What charts, diagrams, or pictures might you include?

3. Design a job aid that you could train your course participants to use eg, a checklist, a process flowchart, etc.

5

How to deliver training that engages participants

This chapter describes the different stages in conducting a training course. The key to successful training is participant involvement and we will focus on methods that stimulate mental and physical participation and ensure learning. After describing each stage in a course, we will look at particular situations the trainer may have to handle. In this way we can follow the progress of training and discuss common problem situations associated with each stage.

Prepare to train

Preparation is a vital stage in any kind of training and thorough preparation will do much to ensure the success of a training session. This is true not only for the new trainer, but for the experienced trainer as well.

Some people think that if the trainer is experienced and has conducted a course many times before, then not much preparation is necessary. With a group of

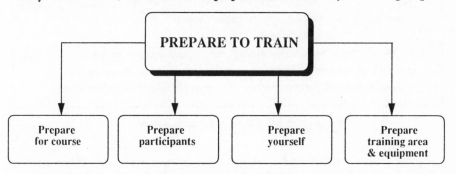

Figure 5.1 *Prepare to train*

Course preparation checklist

Course title: _____

Trainer: _____ Number of participants: _____

Training site: _____ Date(s) of course:_____

Check (✓) when a task is completed. If a task is not applicable, put NA.

Prepare for course (1 week before)

☐ Confirm/check main training room reservation
☐ Confirm/check team or syndicate room reservations
☐ Make your own or participants' travel arrangements
☐ Make refreshment and lunch arrangements

Prepare participants (1 week to 2 days before)

☐ Confirm enrolment and course dates/time/location
☐ Inform them of travel/accommodation arrangements
☐ Send out pre-course tasks – readings, questionnaires, etc.
☐ Inform them of required course preparation
☐ Prepare them for active participation – refer to objectives/activities

Prepare yourself (2 days to 1 day before)

☐ Review and adapt trainer guide to course participants
☐ Prepare and review participant handbook
☐ Prepare flipchart and other visual aids
☐ Review list of participants and decide size and division of groups
☐ If co-training, meet to review course and division of responsibilities

Prepare training area and equipment (1 day before)

☐ Set up the room – seating arrangements, etc.
☐ Set up and check equipment
☐ Check films, videos, slides, transparencies and prepare to use
☐ Check for additional materials – masking tape, pens, handouts, etc.
☐ Distribute participant materials – name plates, handbooks, paper, etc.

Figure 5.2 *Course preparation checklist*

participants that the trainer knows and has worked with before, there may be some validity in this argument. In many training situations though you will not have met the participants before, you may be conducting a new course, or training in a different place or room than usual. Preparation is essential, and a preparation checklist such as Figure 5.2 can save you trying to remember things, prevent the omission of important steps, and ensure that participants are prepared for the course. Thorough preparation will also make you feel more confident at the start of training and help you create a welcoming learning environment. Let's look at these preparation steps on the checklist in a little more detail.

Prepare for the course

Someone else – the registrar or training coordinator – may organize and check on these arrangements for you, but it is often necessary for you to double-check. The reservation of appropriate rooms is particularly important because the area where the course will be conducted influences the choice and organization of activities. A small room may impede the separation necessary for group work, while too large a room may cause groups to feel detached from the trainer and each other. The lack of a small team room in addition to the main training area can also greatly detract from the effectiveness of a course. If only one room is available, this limits the opportunities for team activities or individual consultations eg, the participant watching a recording of his or her videotaped presentation and receiving private feedback from one of the trainers.

A training session also gets off to a bad start if arrangements have not been made properly. Participants' problems with accommodation can take up the time needed for preparation; late arrivals due to faulty travel arrangements or difficulties in locating the room can disrupt your introduction and distract participants; and many an afternoon session has been spoiled by poor luncheon arrangements.

Prepare participants

Again the registrar or training coordinator may confirm participation. It helps a course to get off to a good start however, if the trainer personally contacts participants and confirms the date, time and location of the training. Confusion over times and location can not only disrupt your introductory activities, but embarrass late participants and lead them to make a poor start. Other purposes of this personal contact are to spark participants' interest, encourage them to prepare and, if necessary bring along work materials. In the effort to link training as closely as possible to the jobs people actually do, trainers increasingly require participants to bring along work materials or tasks – for example, materials for a demonstration or presentation, the data for an actual report, etc. Letting participants know about the course beforehand also alerts you to, and can reduce problems caused by, a discrepancy between training objectives and participant expectations.

Prepare yourself

When you're preparing to conduct a course it's best to get logistical and material

MATERIALS PACKING CHECKLIST

ITEM \ DATE									
1 List of participants									
2 Trainer's Guide									
3 Participant Handbooks									
4 Participant handouts									
5 Flipchart									
6 Flipchart markers									
7 Pointer									
8 OHTs									
9 OHP pens									
10 Slides									
11 Video /Film									
12 Name plates									
13 Notepaper									
14 Pencils /pens									
15 Masking tape									
16									

The empty row is for any additional item

Figure 5.3 *Materials packing checklist*

preparations out of the way first; then you can concentrate on preparing yourself mentally. The day before a training session you should prepare or check your flipchart, participant handbooks, overhead transparencies and other materials. This is vital, particularly if you are conducting a course away from your own work site. The materials packing checklist in Figure 5.3, was designed for these off-site courses, what the Americans call 'dog and pony shows'.

If you are conducting the course with someone else, discuss the programme beforehand with your co-trainer. Decide which particular activities you will handle and what your particular roles will be. For example, one trainer may deal with the presentation elements, the other with the discussions and group activities. As you go through your course outline, you need to indicate, generally by initials, who will take responsibility for each activity (see section on co-training at the end of this chapter).

Whether you're co-training or conducting the course by yourself, one of the decisions you need to make is how to divide the participants for group work. Group work provides a medium for participants to learn from each other; you need to consider what type of division will offer the most productive learning environment. Because of the training objectives you may want the groups to be divided on departmental or job lines. For example, you may have different problems or tasks for different organizations – in a course on business meetings the meeting tasks and role-plays may be slightly tailored to particular departments. On the other hand, you may want to mix participants and avoid putting people from the same unit or department together. One of the things people look forward to in attending a course is to get a break from the same department, same faces, same views, same old problems. Working with people from their own department can detract from participants' enjoyment and the creativity of the group. It may also lead to conflict and disruption when feelings which are suppressed in the work environment are set free in the 'safe setting' which a training session often provides.

The most important preparation step is to review the course material in the trainer's guide and tailor it as much as possible to the particular audience. Mentally rehearse the presentation of the course and the activities. Try to think like a participant – what questions might be asked, what problems might arise? For those participants who are likely to be unfamiliar with the content, you will need to provide frequent clarification and review, allow additional time for discussion and practice and avoid information 'overload'. You'll need to look at the agenda and activities and allow for some 'slippage'. If the participants are experienced or familiar with the content though, you will need to ask more difficult questions, provide more challenging tasks and perhaps present additional information on current developments in this area.

Check your agenda and activities and perhaps prepare supplementary material or activities. In this way every training course is different, no matter how many times you have conducted it before. The complex of interactions between you and participants, the participants and the training materials, and the participants with each other makes each course a new one.

Prepare the training area and equipment

Well before the session starts you should set up the room, test the equipment, check the lighting and whether you can adjust it eg, for showing a videotape. You should also check the ventilation – a room that is stuffy or very warm may lull participants to sleep, especially if the trainer lectures much of the time.

An important factor in these preparations is the arrangement of tables and chairs. Some trainers unthinkingly accept a room as it was left by the previous occupant. However, it is important to decide what type of layout is appropriate to your course. The way you arrange the furniture communicates a message to participants and tells them what kind of course this is going to be. The furniture arrangement depends on:

■ the number of participants in the session;
■ the different types of training activities;
■ the formality of the course;
■ how much control the trainer wants over the session.

The diagrams in Figure 5.4 indicate the most common seating arrangements. Rows of tables and chairs indicate a *formal conference* or *lecture session* where large numbers of people need to be accommodated and not much participation is expected. This arrangement provides high trainer control and there is a lack of opportunity for people to interact. If the tables and chairs are in straight rows this tends to create a school classroom atmosphere. If set out in the form of an amphitheatre, this creates a university lecture atmosphere. Quite often with these formal conference or lecture arrangements the trainers are some distance from participants, behind tables or a podium. This reduces participation and people in the back rows are even less likely to participate than those in the front. If you want some participation in this setting, you need to encourage and provide a mechanism for it. For example, you might ask a question and have people discuss it in pairs or triads and then report; you might provide a question and answer period and encourage people from the back to contribute.

The rather formal *u-shape* or more informal *modified-u* are mainly used for courses which involve trainer and media presentation, demonstration and question and answer sessions. Although somewhat formal, the u-shape does allow for discussion and question and answer between participants. It also allows you to walk into and move about the 'u' to increase your eye contact with participants and encourage involvement. Participants at the rear of the 'u' may however be far from the screen, flipchart, or video. Small group work within the training room may also be difficult to set up, and you may need to move the furniture to provide the necessary separation of groups.

Another arrangement that can be used is the *complete square* or *rectangle*. This indicates a small conference or meeting style format where you can function not only as a trainer, but as a member of the meeting. The number of places around the square or rectangle is the number of participants plus the number of trainers. There is no *operating end* and the trainers take the empty seats when the participants have selected theirs.

Tables set out in *cabaret style* or *chevron style* indicate an emphasis on group work and not much formal trainer presentation. They encourage an informal atmos-

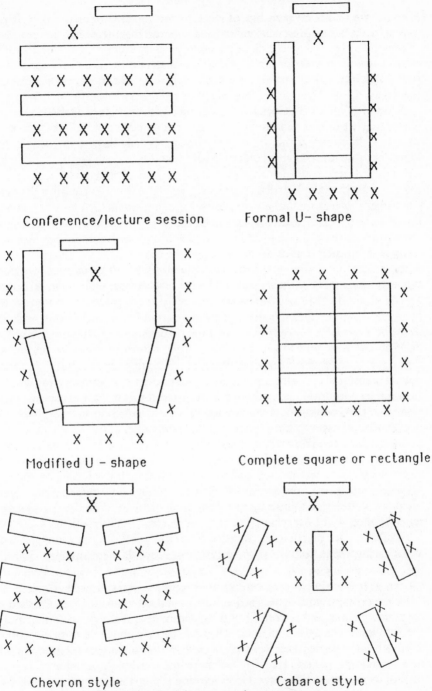

Figure 5.4 *Training room seating arrangements*

phere, a free and open exchange of ideas, where you can circulate freely. If you have to make a long presentation however, these arrangements may lead to a lack of attention among some individuals and side conversations may develop. The cabaret and chevron styles put the emphasis on the trainer as a facilitator and on participant interaction, so they have become, perhaps, the most popular arrangements.

Another point to consider here is whether you want participants to choose where they sit or not. Communication and the dynamics of the course may be adversely affected if, at the beginning, participants only sit with the people they know, or those from the same unit or department. One way to ensure a 'mix' from the start is to write out the participant name cards in advance and place them on the tables before people arrive. That way if you have four people from the same department, you can split them up and perhaps have one in each group. Not only do you and the participants benefit from the 'mix', but you avoid that 'clique' atmosphere at the beginning, and the dangers of a group injecting their negative feelings about their unit or department into the course.

As well as considering where the participants will be, consider your own position at the beginning of the session and for the first activity. Will you stand behind a podium; sit in a chair with no barrier between you and participants; stand at the front and move around a little? During the participant introductions, will you move backwards and forwards towards the participants? Will you first take one position and then shift to another? Your answers to these questions depend on the atmosphere you want to create, the nature of the first activity, and what makes you feel comfortable. Using a podium provides a degree of formality and emphasizes trainer authority. The podium is appropriate for formal presentations: occasions like the opening of a conference or a staff induction course which the department manager might introduce. On the other hand, sitting in a chair with no barrier between you and participants indicates an informal relaxed approach and encourages discussion. If you choose to stand at the front and move around, the atmosphere is less relaxed and more purposeful; in particular, by moving towards participants you demand their contributions and involvement. Quite often you will decide to take up one position in order to make the introductory remarks, then shift to another position for the participant introductions.

Finally, in your preparation you need to go to the back of the room and look at the arrangement from the participants' perspective. Is there anything distracting? Will everyone be able to see the flipchart, the overhead projector screen, the trainer? Is this setting as business-like or attractive as you can make it?

By the time the participants arrive, you should be comfortably established in the training room and in control of the environment. If the room is prepared – the furniture arranged, equipment checked, participant handbooks and name cards set out – participants will feel themselves entering a purposeful and businesslike training session. They will feel more interested in the training and confident of its usefulness. The fact that everything is prepared and the possibility of mishaps has been virtually eliminated, will certainly make you feel more confident. You will be ready to play the gracious host(ess) and conduct a successful training session.

Introduce the course

Anxiety or stage fright can at times affect the most seasoned trainer. A certain amount of anxiety can be useful – it spurs you to prepare well and gets the adrenalin going for a stimulating training course. At times though, particularly during a pilot session, facing a high status or difficult group, or if you're a new trainer, the anxiety may be suddenly disabling. You feel nervous; your throat dries; you want to avoid eye contact with participants; you are afraid your mind will go blank. Here are some ways of reducing anxiety and making a confident start

Confidence boosters

- Avoid the risk of 'drying up' by having a jug of water and a glass at the front of the room.
- Reduce the physical and mental distance between you and participants by meeting and shaking hands with them as they enter. Put yourself and them at ease with a few questions about their journey, mutual acquaintances, your last visit to the participant's department, etc. Besides dissipating your own anxiety, this establishes a warm welcoming climate.
- Deal with administrative details, such as checking attendance on the participant list with each person individually. This gives you an opportunity to speak to everyone and time for participants to settle. Ensure also that each participant writes his or her name down on a name card if you have not already done it. One of the most critical aspects of climate-setting is that every face should be attached to a name as soon as possible – by the trainer as well as by other participants. If you repeat the participant's name after he or she has given it, you are less likely to forget it. There is nothing more unnerving for a trainer than to forget a participant's name or confuse him or her with another person.
- If you are still nervous, breathe in deeply several times before you start to speak. Make sure that your opening comments come out strongly.
- 'Sweep' the room with your eyes and make eye contact with each participant. This will reduce your anxiety and from the participants' viewpoint, convey a definite air of command and confidence – make them feel you are speaking personally to them. Avoid focusing on just one friendly-looking participant or at a far point in the room.
- Begin speaking in a clear deliberate way. Make every effort not to rush the first few minutes; if you use a carefully measured pause during this period, it can be highly effective. Many trainers, because of their nervousness, start speaking at too rapid a pace and their voice becomes high-pitched. The participants

begin to feel left behind and anxious – this is conveyed through their expressions – and the trainer becomes even more nervous. If you feel this happening, slow down and lend authority to what you say by lowering your pitch.

■ Continue 'sweeping' the audience with your eyes, occasionally focusing on one person. This not only gives you platform presence, but builds rapport with participants.

■ Avoid 'closed' or tense body positions and open up through the use of gesture, facial expression and variety of tone and pitch. Move around a little to release tension; it helps to develop rapport if you move towards participants.

■ Avoid at all costs beginning in an apologetic or self-deprecating tone. If you show a lack of confidence in conducting the course and achieving the course objectives, then you lose credibility.

First steps

When you are working with groups you need a good solid introduction to gain interest and keep it. Here are some of the things you should do at the beginning.

Announce the title of the course

This should also be on the cover or first page of the flipchart. It is surprising how many people are sent to courses not knowing what the title or topic is. Make sure your participants know from the beginning.

Introduce yourself

Tell the participants who you are and what your role is – some details of your experience with the company and of the course topic will add to your credibility. Try to relax the atmosphere with some self-disclosure or amusing comments. Your own introduction should provide a model for the introductions participants will make later.

Explain administrative arrangements

Here you can let participants know about breaks, lunch arrangements, the rules on smoking, where and when participants can collect messages or make telephone calls.

Introduce the course briefly

Describe the employee needs that led to the course, why management felt the training was necessary, and any other details that will help answer the participant question, ' Why am I here?'. Explain the relevance of the course to participants' job performance – how frequently they need to use particular information or a skill and how critical it is. Here you are concerned with motivating participants and answering their as yet unspoken question, 'What's in it for me?'. Satisfying this question early on and convincing participants of the relevance of this training to their jobs, futures, or personal lives, is very important for motivation.

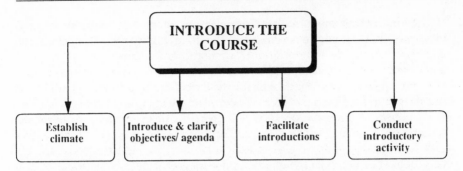

Figure 5.5 *Introduce the course*

Introduce and clarify the course objectives and agenda

Provide clear statements of intent: identify what will be discussed, and if necessary what will not be discussed. If there is going to be some kind of test or evaluation, let them know – this is not only fair to them but will raise the level of attention and learning. Here are some examples of different types of introduction and their area of focus:

Today we will first... (overview)
Do you remember that last week.. (context)
By the end of this session you will be able to... (objectives)
This session deals with one of the most critical... (What's in it for me)
At the end of this session we will assess... (evaluation).

The course objectives and agenda may be written up on pages of the flipchart but it is often useful to include them as the first page in the participant's handbook. Emphasize how the agenda and the training activities are geared to the achievement of objectives – what participants should be able to do by the end of the course. Emphasize also that these are *participant objectives*, not trainer objectives. Indeed the focus of the training is on what they, the participants, do rather than on what you will do. Never undermine yourself and the course by saying things like 'Hopefully we'll do this' or 'If we've got time, we'll do this'. As far as participants are concerned, you are responsible for the organization and pacing of the session.

Facilitate introductions

Now you are concerned with breaking the ice, 'warming up' participants and establishing a comfortable atmosphere. One way to start the introductions is to list questions on the flipchart: name, department, job, then a topic question that elicits what experience participants have on the course topic and what their expectations are. For a course on business meetings, you might ask participants to give information on the business meetings they attend and comment on their effectiveness.

Then individuals can introduce themselves, or better still, after a short interview, introduce the person next to them. Listen carefully to the introduction, and add your own comments or additional questions; show interest in the participants and their experience and, if possible, link their information with the course topic. If a participant uses too much time for the introduction, intervene tactfully and put the group back on track; here, as elsewhere, pacing is important.

Responses to the topic question will give you an opportunity to relate the training to individual work situations. These responses can also be used, with a little further prompting, to elicit participants' attitudes, hidden agendas and expectations. For example, the question on business meetings may reveal general cynicism about the value of meetings, anxiety among some participants about how to 'control' their meetings, and the expectation that this course will provide some simple meeting control strategies. It can be useful to list these responses or participant expectations on the flipchart. This serves several purposes. It indicates the importance you attach to participant responses, allows you to check these responses and expectations against course objectives and helps to identify any discrepancies. If difficult problems arise, the flipchart pages listing participant concerns can be taped up on the training room walls. This activity provides a safety valve and shows that you are keen to deal with people's concerns during the training. This listing of concerns can also be useful when you report to the client or your own management on the course.

Participant introductions also give you a sense of who the 'characters' will be on the course – who you might use to stimulate discussion, who might provide a touch of humour, who might be used as models to start a role-play activity, who might create problems. You can start to 'tune in' to individuals and groups of participants and begin through their comments, facial expressions and body language to experience the course as they do. Specifically, you can use this introductory period to disarm the malcontent, relieve the anxious participant and convince the slow learner that everyone is in this together and there is nothing to fear.

As mentioned earlier, you can speed up or slow down the introduction process through your own physical movement and pace. Sitting in a relaxed position encourages informal leisurely discussion. When you stand up, write on the flipchart, or move around, the process becomes more purposeful and you speed up the activity.

Conduct an introductory activity

At the beginning of a course it is most important for you to create a climate that's conducive to learning. Following the introductions, there may be an ice-breaker activity involving a group or pair exercise and discussion. Providing a discussion so early in the course prevents participants from slipping back into the pupil role they learnt at school; by the same token, it acts as a brake on you falling into the teacher role. By giving participants ample opportunity to express themselves early in the session, you also show respect for their knowledge and experience. You emphasize that you value participation and that participants are expected to contribute. Perhaps most important of all, such discussions provide a safety valve for any frustrations or *hidden agendas* which participants have brought with them to the course. If these feelings are left unexpressed, they might surface unpredictably at critical points and destroy the effectiveness of the training.

In some courses a pre-test or questionnaire might be given at the beginning (see Chapter 4). The scores on this would indicate to participants the extent of their knowledge and what additional information they needed to know. The same test or questionnaire might then be given again at the end of the course. If you choose to use a pre-test or questionnaire, point out that this is a learning tool for participants to diagnose their own learning needs. Try to reduce any fears or sense of threat; one way to do this is to let participants score their own papers and keep their own results.

Common situations

Situation: You wake up on the morning of the course and find that your voice is very weak. You are afraid you will lose your voice completely.
Suggestions: Drink lemon and hot water. Minimize the use of your voice at the start of the course. With some rest, your voice may return before the day is out. Do as much group and participative work as possible. Assign group leaders and have a participant collect results from the groups. Use the time during the group work to observe and to make extra flipcharts to help you through. If there is a film or video that deals with the subject, consider showing it even if it is not as good as what you planned to do.

Situation: You don't think you'll be able to remember everything you need to say. You want to read your speech.
Suggestions: If you read your speech, you are ensuring a monotonous and boring training session or presentation. Use notes, handouts, flipchart pages and over-head transparencies to provide your outline and key points as you speak. When you use visual aids in this way as cues, your mind can select words spontaneously. Your voice is naturally more active and interesting because you are continuously thinking and adapting your presentation to the audience.

Situation: You begin to speak but suddenly feel yourself 'drying up'. Your voice starts to quiver and you come to a halt.
Suggestions: Try to relax. Pause and have a sip of water. Take a deep breath and look at a friendly face in the audience. Then start to speak again. Try to smile – this will help you relax and generally connect better to the audience. The audience indeed may not notice the brief interruption – what seems like eternity to you is in reality often only a few seconds. They may take your hesitation as simply a natural pause in the flow of the presentation.

Situation: You started the course 15 minutes ago and the last participant is introducing himself. Suddenly the door opens and your missing participant rushes in. He comes up to you and says his supervisor only told him about the course this morning. How should you handle him and get the session running smoothly again?

Suggestions: Be understanding. Say you are sorry that he did not receive the news until this morning, indicate an empty seat and tell him that the participants are just introducing themselves. Turn your attention to the person who was speaking, apologize and ask him or her to continue. Talk with them for a few minutes and then, having given the newcomer this breathing space, ask him to introduce himself. When selecting an introductory activity, one of your criteria might be that it should be an activity that allows you to integrate newcomers fairly easily.

Situation: You are introducing a course and emphasizing the relevance of the objectives and activities to the participants' jobs. Most of the participants look interested and there are nods as you point out relevance. One participant however is sitting with a rather scornful expression on his face. Suddenly he interrupts and says, 'Look...we're just in from the field. What do you know about what we have to put up with?'.

Suggestions: This questioner is projecting his own anger onto the others. He is defending his own attitude and attacking you by claiming that the other participants feel the same way. They may well not. The question though is a dangerous one because it challenges the credibility of the course and yourself. One of the best ways to respond is to ask the participant to explain his own particular work situation and try to find points of relevance between his work and the training. If the course *does* relate and he has not really understood that, make the relevance apparent without making him look stupid. If the relevance is limited, admit it but indicate how some of the training could help him. If there is no obvious relevance to this participant's job, the course may still be personally useful and he could gain from the knowledge and experience of other participants. Moreover, the participant's supervisor nominated the questioner for the training and there must be reasons for that. Perhaps the supervisor is preparing the employee for new responsibilities or a new post and has not explained this yet. Your contacts and experience in the field are of critical importance here and it is certainly helpful to be able to say that you have visited this man's worksite or one very similar to it. Whatever you do, avoid appearing defensive. Show that you really want to help the participant.

Situation: Right from the beginning of a course on effective supervision it's clear that several participants feel it is a waste of time. They say their bosses should be taking the course instead of them.

Suggestions: Agree that it might be very useful if their bosses did take the course themselves. Participants should tell their managers about the training when they return to their jobs. In this way managers might be encouraged to attend or at least take up some of the ideas from the course. At the same time, people often learn by example. If participants follow the principles and strategies of effective supervision, then they will not only do a better job themselves, but provide a good example for their boss.

This situation raises a critical training issue. Participants may understand, accept and be able to apply the information and skills they have learnt from a course. If there is no support for the new behaviour back on the job however, then participants will either be unable to use the new information and skills, or be frustrated when trying to use them. Here follow-up visits involving meetings with participants and their supervisors are very important. Follow-up provides that critical link between training and on-the-job application. Your visits show organizational support for participants' new behaviour and, by involving their supervisors, increase the chances of employees applying what has been learned. If you conduct follow-ups after the course, it is much easier to respond to participant scepticism.

Use situational training techniques

Many different terms are used to identify the person who conducts a training course. Course leader, presenter, trainer, or facilitator are the most common. The term you use tends to indicate your training philosophy. To some people the term *course leader* sounds rather authoritarian and directive, and *presenter* seems to put too much emphasis on the presentation of course information. *Facilitator*, on the other hand, is a term which suggests that the person conducting the course is mainly there to facilitate the exchange of participant information and experience and to make the course activities run smoothly. A *facilitator* may be appropriate for a seminar, a problem-solving discussion, or a focus group meeting where the training is largely based on participant input. For most courses however where decisions about the objectives, activities, materials and everything else have been made by the person, group, or organization conducting the session, the term *facilitator* seems hardly appropriate.

Trainer is a neutral term encompassing the whole variety of roles played by someone conducting a course. At different times you may be concerned with *task activities;* you will be a *leader* introducing the course and directing activities, or a *presenter* making a formal presentation. At other times you may be concerned with *process activities*. You will be a *facilitator*, encouraging and stimulating discussion, monitoring and guiding group activities, coaching individual participants as they apply their learning and practise new skills. At other times you might just stand back and observe as participants work through a task or activity and learn from each other and the experience. A trainer therefore needs to be flexible – to adjust roles and styles in response to the requirements of activities, participant needs and responses and the achievement of course objectives. We might call this *situational training* – a parallel to the *situational leadership* approach to management and supervision.

By the end of the course introduction, you should be able to judge the following characteristics of the situation and act accordingly:

■ The level of participants' knowledge or familiarity with the topic – their readi-

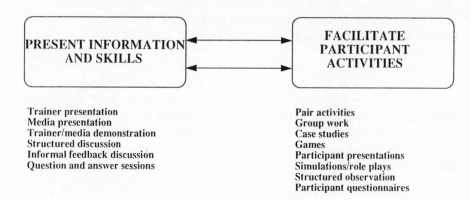

Figure 5.6 *Situational training*

ness to learn in terms of knowledge and skills. With uninformed or inexperienced participants, you need to be more of a *leader* giving information and directions and closely monitoring activities. With informed and experienced participants however, you are more of a *facilitator* and can use participants as a resource, eliciting their knowledge and experience and unobtrusively guiding them through the activities.

■ The maturity of individual participants. Maturity here involves participants' attitudes to the topic, the objectives, the trainer and their emotional readiness to learn. This is not maturity or immaturity in a total sense but in relation to the particular course material. It is common for there to be great differences in maturity between participants in relation to a course. You need to lead, give individual guidance and direction to 'immature' participants. With more 'mature' participants however, you can be less directive and behave as a *facilitator*. You can draw out these participants' ideas and experiences for the benefit of the group and delegate responsibilities to them eg, leadership of groups, reporting responsibilities, role-play modelling.

Situational training means therefore that you continuously adjust to the task and process requirements of the course and the various, changing, individual needs of participants. Make any necessary adjustments to the activities and to your own training style as the course progresses. Throughout, you should demonstrate a concern for the participants and their individual learning: balance a concern for people with a concern for achieving the objectives and tasks at hand.

Present information/skills

When you conduct a training course you usually present new information or skills. Course presentation activities might include:

- Presentation or demonstration by the trainer
- Presentation or demonstration through media
- Structured discussion
- Informal feedback discussions
- Question and answer sessions.

Presentation or demonstration by the trainer

For better or worse, you tend to be judged by your employers and by course participants on your presentation skills. This is the highly visible part of your work and the improvement of presentation skills is something that both new and experienced trainers are always working on. Information and advice for improvement can come from observing other trainers' presentations, videotaping some of your own presentations, asking colleagues to observe and give feedback and of course feedback from your participants.

The effectiveness of a presentation is usually related to the success with which it follows the KISS principle. This acronym is variously interpreted as Keep It Short and Simple, or more colloquially, Keep It Simple, Stupid. The inexperienced trainer tends to focus on the content of a presentation, making sure that nothing is omitted and every detail included. He or she may be tempted to digress either through interest, a wish to show off knowledge, or a mistaken fear of 'short-changing' participants. The methods to be used in the presentation and transmission of the content then tend to be treated as an afterthought and participants stay silent, confused and suffering from 'information overload'. The experienced trainer, however, focuses on content and methods together and breaks the presentation up into meaningful segments. He or she tries to keep the participants mentally and physically active by avoiding long sessions of trainer talk and using the information– activity– report cycle. The trainer constantly puts himself or herself in the place of participants coming into contact with this material or experiencing these activities for the first time.

Books on how to make presentations often advise: 'Tell them what you're going to say, say it, then tell them what you've said'. In terms of sequence you might provide an overview to emphasize the main points of the presentation and their relationship with each other. After presenting 'the big picture' you can provide the details necessary for understanding or implementing each of the main points in turn. Here you should focus on those details that participants will *need to know*. The inclusion of *nice to know* details depends on the time available and what the participants *want* to know. If they want more details, this might be achieved through a question and answer session; a discussion at the end of the presentation, or through back-up resources such as reprints of articles. Finally, you should review the main points of the presentation and lead into the question and answer or discussion session.

The effective use of visual aids can simplify a presentation and strengthen both the trainer's and participants' sense of logical sequence. Presentations are often structured through the use of overhead transparencies, slides, or a succession of video clips with the trainer's voice providing focus and continuity. Visual aids clarify and reinforce the information you present and give additional variety and interest to the presentation. As described in Chapter 4, they can greatly increase a speaker's persuasiveness – sales and business presenters would not spend the time and money on them otherwise. Decide whether to allow questions or not during a particular presentation. Generally this depends on the presentation length – a long presentation may need to be broken up by questions and some discussion. With short presentations, you can ask participants to note down their points and questions and save them until the end. Sometimes a presentation may, despite your best efforts, be information-packed and fairly complex; for example, the introduction of a new project. Questions during the presentation may lead to confusion, with the participants focusing on small details rather than getting the big picture first. In this situation it is best to remind participants that you are providing an overview and will be focusing on the main points. Encourage them to make notes and save their questions about the details until later.

One popular presentation technique is the Socratic method where the trainer alternately uses questions and explanation to present the information. This technique is often used in conjunction with a flipchart build-up. The trainer asks a question and elicits the first main point. He or she elicits more detail from the participants if possible, but if not adds the detailed information. The trainer then elicits the next point through a question, and so on. If participants can't answer then the trainer provides the information. This approach follows the proposition – *If you think they know it or know part of it, get it from them by asking questions*. Major advantages of this technique are that it involves participants, uses their knowledge and experience – and can create a dynamic learning atmosphere.

When a course involves skill training, you can best present the skill by demonstrating it. Most people need to see a skill actually being demonstrated step-by-step and you need to give at least one demonstration of the skill before asking participants to practise. Demonstrations can of course also provide 'models' for skills such as interviewing, interpersonal communication, or coaching. A demonstration by the trainer and one of the participants – for example on corrective coaching – may therefore be used to start a role-play sequence.

Presentation or demonstration through media

Sometimes the major or an important part of a presentation is made through the use of media: film, videotape, or slides. It is undesirable for participants to slip into the passive role of just 'watching TV' however. The best way of avoiding this is to make the media presentation as interactive as possible; this can be achieved quite easily in the following way:

■ Introduce the film or video and perhaps a task participants should perform while watching eg, making notes on particular points, preparing to answer some questions afterwards, looking out for specific things that will be discussed later.

■ Show the film or video. A short video or film may be run straight through but you may wish to pause or stop at certain points for discussion. With a long video, provide breaks for discussion.

■ Follow-up. Here there may be a discussion of critical points in the film or video. You might ask participants to work individually, in pairs, or in groups on a worksheet. Whether you decide to have individual, pair, or group work depends on the difficulty of the task, the demands of task variety, or the amount of time you have for reporting. For example, you may have planned that completion of a video worksheet should be an individual activity. If you run short of time or if the participants have difficulty with the material, you may feel that at this stage they need to work together more. You decide to make completing the worksheet a group activity with one representative from each group reporting. This speeds up completion of the task, increases participant interaction and reduces reporting time.

When a course involves skills training, you might also use a video to demonstrate how to do a task or to present a model. In a presentation skills course you might use a video recording of a previous participant giving a presentation. This would demonstrate what is required and as long as the presentation is not too perfect, encourage your current participants.

Structured discussion

We have seen how discussion can be used as an ice-breaking activity and an opportunity for participants to 'let off steam' about the training topic. We have also seen how these start-up discussions can set the tone of participant involvement and enable you to identify particular types of participant early in the training session. Discussion can of course also be an important means of presenting information and *structured discussions* are formal discussions which are included in the agenda or in the trainer's outline. These discussions are usually structured by oral or written questions and may involve a flip-chart build-up by the trainer based on participants' responses, or completion of particular tasks or worksheets.

The discussion of pre-course reading material is a good example of a structured discussion. In a session on business meetings information on meetings can be presented through the pre-course reading and questions which are sent to participants in advance. After the introductory activity, you might give participants ten minutes to review the reading and prepare to answer the questions. Then, during the discussion, these written questions and your oral follow-up questions can guide participants to consider and apply the information on business meetings to their own meetings and work situation. This questioning also draws out participants' ideas and experience on this topic. The final question on the pre-course reading might be: 'Based on this article and the discussion so far, what do you think are the principles that contribute to effective meetings?'. You might write responses to the question on the flipchart and use this as a means of summarizing the discussion. In this way discussion is structured and provides a means of presenting, eliciting, clarifying and applying new information.

Because structured discussion is flexible and can be adjusted to participant needs (you might spend more time on one question than others because of participant responses) and includes comprehension checks, it can be a very effective means of presentation. As it involves participants and allows for 'give and take' between you and them, the structured discussion method is also particularly useful in situations where changes in attitude are required or potential hostility needs to be overcome.

Structured discussion can also be a means of generating action plans or action items for when participants get back to their jobs. If action items are going to be generated through the discussion, you or preferably one of the participants might record these items on the flipchart.

Discussion involves you in both *task-oriented behaviour* (giving and asking for information, synthesizing ideas, summarizing, clarifying and expanding) and *process-oriented behaviour* (maintaining a friendly atmosphere, keeping communication channels open, encouraging reserved participants, restraining the voluble). You will need to shift from one to the other depending on the progress of the discussion.

Informal feedback discussions

These are discussions which are not included in the agenda and may be held at any time through the course to check participant understanding and encourage involvement. In particular, you can use them at the end of activities to discuss the results and the applications of an exercise. The content and length of these discussions depends on the activity, how you feel the session is progressing and on the time available.

Plan and structure these informal discussions carefully and pay attention to timing. An ever-present danger with discussion is that it goes on too long, the articulate participants dominate, and you yourself become too involved either intellectually or emotionally. In this situation the less articulate participants often lose the thread of the discussion, retreat into themselves, and think, 'This isn't for me!'. At this point your questioning and response techniques are critical.

Skilled trainers spend a lot of time asking questions and again, as in the structured discussion, you can guide participants through your use of questions. *Open questions* asking for participant feelings, opinions or experience can open up the discussion and lead to lengthy exchanges, not only between yourself and participants, but between participants themselves. *Closed questions* which focus purely on the results or information gained from the activity can be used to control the discussion and, if necessary, bring it to an end.

In the same way your responses can encourage or regulate the discussion. Ways of encouraging participant responses include establishing eye contact, nodding, moving or leaning forward to listen more closely, and verbal lubricators like 'I see', 'Ah-ah', 'That's interesting', 'Go on' and 'Can you tell us more about that?'. On the other hand, communication regulators or 'stoppers' include looking away or down at your notes, and verbal stoppers like an emphatic 'OK', 'Yes, but...', 'Can we move on to...', 'Well, I'm not sure I agree with you on...', and 'I think other people may feel differently'.

Moving out of the discussion can also sometimes be difficult, especially if a few participants have 'got the bit between their teeth'. Watch for signs of restlessness among participants and end the discussion while interest is still high. You also need to plan your transitions, your bridges into the next activity in advance. Your last question or comments should encourage participant responses that lead into the next activity.

Question and answer sessions

These sessions are often held after a formal presentation activity. An important part of your preparation for a course which involves a question and answer sequence is to prepare a list of questions which might be asked. It is helpful if you can ask a colleague to provide additional, preferably difficult, questions.

When dealing with a new or complex topic, you may have a specialist present to handle detailed technical questions. The specialist may also, through the meeting, improve his or her contact with the participants who are implementing the new project, procedure or process. Prepare the specialist fully, not just for questions but for possible hostility. New projects or processes are not universally welcome and specialists are not always good presenters. A *dry-run* of the specialist's presentation, with you asking some difficult or hostile questions, may be necessary.

Common situations

Situation: You are making a presentation but one of the participants interrupts to ask a question. The annoying thing is that the question relates to something you are about to come to. If this person waited a few moments, she would receive the answer to her question.
Suggestions: This interruption may be a danger sign indicating that your presentation is too long or that many questions are being left unanswered. It may be time for you to stop, answer the question, and ask if anyone else has questions at this point. If your presentation is not long however, stop, smile, and tell the participant that you are just about to come to that point. If she waits, you hope to deal with most questions and there will be time at the end of the presentation for a question and answer session.

Situation: You have just completed the presentation part of the course and are responding to questions. Suddenly a participant who has been sitting at the back with his arms folded and a sceptical expression on his face speaks up: 'This sounds very well here, but it won't work'. There are nods and looks of agreement from other participants.

Suggestions: Ask questions to define why 'it won't work'. Avoid being defensive and show you are anxious to help this participant in his work situation. Sometimes participants are honestly unable to implement the information and skills they acquire from a training session, but more often they *can* do something. Blanket dismissal of the material as 'unpractical in my situation' is often an excuse. The participant may not really want to change his, or what he believes is his department's, way of doing business.

Situation: It's the first day of a five-day course. One participant arrived late, came back late after the coffee break and is late again after lunch. You are ten minutes into the afternoon session and are just introducing a videotape when he strolls in.

Suggestions: You should have tackled this issue after the coffee break when he came late for the second time. Now he's disrupting the session again. You can not do anything publicly, but take him aside either during a group activity or at the beginning of the next break to ask him why he was late on three occasions. Tell him that it is not only a problem for you, but for the other participants as well – he is holding up the training. Ask him if he anticipates any further delays. If so, suggest he takes the course at another time because he will not meet the course objectives and will therefore fail to complete. Tell him that his supervisor will also need to be contacted about this! At that stage the participant will probably apologize.

Situation: You are conducting a discussion and participants are relating the ideas in the course to their jobs. One participant begins to talk about his job but soon begins to criticize his supervisor and the way the department operates. Other participants agree with him and start to suggest that you might do something about this work situation. The additional discussion means that you are already ten minutes behind on your schedule.

Suggestions: Show understanding of the participants' concerns, but explain that you are not prepared to support or criticize someone who is not present to put his or her own case. Indicate your own limitations – you can only guide and help the people who come along to courses. The hope is that training like this will make the participants better supervisors or employees themselves and improve the company's operation. If you are conducting follow-up after the course, you can refer to this as a way of gaining supervisors' support and helping participants apply their learning. Then return to the topic of the discussion, summarize the relevant points and arguments so far, and ask for closing comments. Close the discussion. Indicate the time constraints and that there is still a lot of important ground to cover. If a coffee break is due, it is often useful to hold it after a discussion. Any contentious or individual issues can be dealt with informally in the break and participants can let off steam. If a break is not due after a discussion, try to schedule an attention-grabbing change of activity – a video exercise, a group task, or a role-play. Indeed one of the most important things to consider in setting your agenda is how you are going to conclude a discussion and what should follow it. When problems emerge in a training session it is usually during a discussion – participants need to be allowed to vent their concerns, but at the same time a few participants should not be allowed to disrupt the course.

Situation: You are conducting a discussion and one participant who has hardly spoken so far disagrees strongly with an important point that you make. There seems to be an emotional force behind her disagreement.

Suggestions: You need to treat the participant's disagreement as a positive and welcome contribution. Establish eye contact, smile, nod and use encouraging phrases and lubricators, like 'I see', 'Ah-ah', 'Go on', 'Please tell us more about that'. These will defuse the emotional force which may be a result of the participant not having spoken much and being unsure of the response she will get. Ask her to clarify or amplify what she has said and use additional questions to assess the level of disagreement. Quite often the disagreement will be the result of misunderstanding, based on a difference of emphasis, or relate to another aspect of the topic. Sometimes the outburst may be the result of frustration at not having contributed much so far and a desire for attention. If the disagreement relates to critical points in the course material or approach however, this needs to be discussed openly. You should try to find out if other participants have similar views but are not expressing them.

If you finally disagree with the participant's idea or comment make it clear that you are rejecting the viewpoint not the participant. Try to involve her even more in the discussion and course activities.

A general point here is that you should try to treat differences constructively – as interesting, as an opportunity to discuss different perspectives and as contributing to the success of training. Do not treat differences as interruptions getting in the way of your training session, as an expression of negative attitudes, or as hostile. If you treat differences positively, this contributes to the creative dynamics, variety and interest of the course. Participants become more involved and as a result can learn more.

Facilitate participant activities

Trainers and training courses tend to provide a lot of time for the transmission and discussion of information. Quite often though there is insufficient time for participant activities – the discovery, assimilation, practice, rehearsal or application of the knowledge or skills being learned. In Chapter 3, we discussed the importance of providing sufficient time for participant activities in the course design process. During the training however, you should avoid having participant activity time 'eaten up' by elaborations on the presentation, long discussions of abstract concepts, or the interesting digressions people sometimes employ to avoid having the 'spotlight' focused on their own activity. As far as possible, keep the discovery, practice, or application periods for those specific purposes; every participant should have time and opportunity to find out things, work with the training materials, and try out what he or she has learned. Time indeed is critical with all participant activities and you need to allow enough time for a task to be completed – not too much though, or the pace and momentum of the course may be lost.

In Chapter 3 we looked at the role of participant activities in training courses and at different types of activity, including structured experiences. That chapter focused on describing the types of activity or 'experience' and reasons for selecting or developing a particular type. The focus in this chapter, however, will be on the factors you need to consider when conducting a particular activity.

Preparation

One of the most important preparation concerns is how long a participant activity or experience will take and what difficulties might arise in the activity. Leave room for flexibility in timing to allow for different types of participants; participant maturity is an important consideration here. This is why it is so important to have a *dry-run* or see another trainer conduct the activity. If *you* have questions or doubts about a particular activity, try to solve the problems and settle any doubts *before* the actual training course.

Starting

Give participants a broad overview of the activity and then provide any further instruction in small parts. You should avoid excessive instruction and explanation – participants probably will not retain the information and you may bore them with the activity before it starts. It is fairly easy for most people to keep three items in mind at once, so it is often useful to limit the instructions for any one part of the activity to three points. These might be given on the task sheet or written up on the flipchart at the appropriate time.

Conducting

Make sure that everyone knows what they are doing and has something to do. Monitor the activity and participate whenever it seems appropriate.

Focus on learning

Try to turn everything that happens into a learning experience. Do not prevent participants from making mistakes unless the value of the whole activity would be destroyed if you did not intervene. People sometimes learn most from their mistakes and often 'mistakes' can make the activity and the training more productive. After the activity, and perhaps at appropriate points during it, help participants prepare to transfer their learning to personal or job situations. Participant activities during a course might include:

- Pair activities
- Group work
- Case studies
- Games
- Participant presentations or demonstrations
- Simulations and role plays
- Structured observation
- Participant questionnaires.

Pair activities

In situations where individuals might have some difficulty with a task or where you feel more participant interaction is required, then a task might be made into a pair activity. We have already seen how participants can be paired to introduce each other, or complete a video worksheet together. In order to overcome the sometimes threatening aspects of public role-play, participant role-plays can also be turned into a pair activities with an observer completing an observation sheet and discussing this with the pair afterwards. The observer then becomes a participant and so the roles are rotated.

Group work

Group activities ensure that participants learn from each other through the exchange of information and experience, and that they stay active and involved. Participants therefore not only function as an information resource but as a source of energy and enable you to conserve your own voice and energy. This becomes particularly important in a long course. In order to ensure the effectiveness of group activities you need to pay attention to the following factors.

Group shifting and size

There are several ways to divide participants up into working groups; here are two:

- The pre-planned method. Prior to the activity, select the participants to make up balanced groups. This way you can mix knowledgeable or experienced people with those who are less knowledgeable or experienced. Alternatively, depending on your objectives, you can divide groups up on the basis of departments or jobs. List the groups on the flipchart or place the selected name cards at group tables.
- The random method. After counting the number of participants, decide on the number of groups and the size of each group. For example if there are 18 participants and you want three groups, you can count off groups of six or

number them off, 'One, two, three. One, two, three' etc. 'All the Ones here, the Twos there, and the Threes in this corner.'

Particularly during a long training course, you might also shift the composition of the working groups. Do not be afraid to let participants move about – physical movement as people shift from one group to another often enlivens participants and the training session. By shifting group composition you also encourage each person to come into contact with all the other participants and prevent them being 'saddled' with the same people they worked with last time. On the other hand, when you shift the composition of groups it means that it takes longer for them to settle down and start working effectively.

Limit the size of your groups. With seven or more people in a group, problems of involvement can arise – more reserved participants retreat into themselves and let the more assertive take over. Problems of communication within the group can also arise with larger groups.

Preparation of participants

Make sure that participants know the precise objectives of the group activity. Your directions for group work should always state exactly what you want people to do; how you suggest they might do it; what results, outcomes or products are expected; and how much time they have to complete the activity. It is useful to write the objectives and directions for the activity on the flipchart and they may also be included on a task sheet. Some people understand what they *see* better than what they *hear*, and if any confusion arises during an activity, participants have the instructions for reference. Any task sheet, whether it is in the participant handbook or distributed as a handout, should be capable of standing alone.

If it seems there might be difficulties, give participants an example of the type of response required. Several examples may be necessary, especially when participants are unused to group problem solving or staff training courses.

Set a brisk pace with realistic but challenging time limits. There is a tendency among trainers to underestimate the time participants need to complete a task – the *dry-run* and the *pilot* presentation will probably indicate that you need a little more time. Avoid giving too much time though – you don't want participants to take it easy or become bored waiting for others to finish.

Provide a flipchart which the group can use for planning, to structure their work, or to record their findings. If groups are working in the main training room, they should have one flipchart each. If groups are working in team rooms, they can bring back the flipchart pages with their findings to the main training room. They can then tape these pages to the walls. This makes it easier for groups to report, for an observer to make comments, and for you to comment as well.

Remember to leave enough time for reporting – for group representatives to report on the outcomes of group activity – and for general discussion. You will need to increase this time if observers are required to provide 'process' reports on the different groups' activity.

The trainer's role

One of the most critical decisions to make during small group work is when and when not to intervene. Important factors here are the maturity of the group in relation to the task, whether the small group activity is in the main training room or in team rooms, and what stage the group have reached. If the topic or task is non-controversial and the main training room is being used, then you can intervene fairly unobtrusively when necessary. When groups are in team rooms however, your intervention becomes more obtrusive and may threaten the group's independence. The stage the group has reached is also important; you can use noise and activity levels as indicators of how groups are progressing. Five stages in a group activity might be identified:

1. *The start-up* – when the sound level is rather low and subdued. Group members get to know each other, identify the task (usually by quietly reading it), then someone suggests that it's time to start. With a mature group at this stage, you can just monitor at a distance, ensure that the group have no problems and understand what is required. With a less mature group however, you may need to monitor more closely and be ready to assist. If this group is working in a team room, you may need to spend a few minutes with them but try to avoid doing so at the beginning. Whatever the maturity level of the group, they should be allowed time to settle down and make a start on the task.

2. *Analysis and thought-collecting* is also a relatively quiet time. One or two people tend to take the lead at this stage, ask other participants for their ideas and responses, and try to get decisions. Sometimes these decisions are pushed through too quickly and this creates problems later. Sound levels begin to build slowly. With mature groups you should let the group dynamics work and avoid intervening. In immature groups however, confusion over the task or conflict may create problems. In the absence of an internal moderator, you may need to intervene and get the group back 'on task'.

3. *The main working stage* – when noise levels are generally high but fluctuating. There is greater activity: participants standing up to write on the flipchart, collecting or checking resources (if available), engaging in lively discussion. A sense of urgency begins to develop towards the end of this stage as participants recognize deadlines. Again with mature groups you should avoid intervening, except to remind a group of the deadline if they seem to be behind. Immature groups may require more in the way of suggestions and assistance.

4. *Finishing the task* is often characterized by frantic activity as groups try to meet the deadline. When the task is complete, there tends to be a sharp drop in noise levels. Participants relax and begin to chat with each other – the group begins to break up. You should then check on the completion of the task and ensure that each group, its representative, and perhaps the observer

are ready for the report stage. Immature representatives or observers may need some assistance in preparing their reports.

5. *Reporting and evaluating the activity* is the final stage. Mature participants should preferably speak from the front and use the flipchart as a guide. Less mature participants might report from their seats or stand up and use a flipchart in their area of the room. You might ask a few clarifying questions during the reports but avoid 'up-staging' the participants making their brief presentations.

Case studies

Case studies are a popular way of increasing involvement and job relevance by bringing participants face-to-face with real situations and practical problems. Case studies may be produced externally (as in an 'off-the-shelf' training film or video), by the course developer, the trainer, or the participants. In the latter case participants, usually working in pairs or small groups, can use their own experience of the job and real-life problems. When the case studies are completed the pairs or small groups might exchange them and work on their solution. In this way participants are helped with the job they are returning to and the training is seen to be directly applicable to improved job performance.

You need to be particularly skilful in leading discussion at the end of, or during, a case study session. Keep discussion focused on the problems raised by each case study and the decisions that need to be made, but at the same time facilitate a free and informal discussion.

Games

In contrast to role-plays, games are generally viewed as non-threatening and are popular with participants. Trainers also need a change of pace and a well-placed game can stimulate you as well. Games, however, should not be used as a pleasant time-filler merely to while away the final afternoon of a long course. Games should tie in with other activities and a game is often used to synthesize skills learned during a course

Compared to role-plays, games are relatively easy to conduct and do not usually require a great amount of trainer preparation. However, even the most experienced trainer needs to see a game conducted by another trainer before attempting to do it alone. In particular you need to find out what instructions are required, what problems might arise, how long the game takes with different types and sizes of group and how the feedback and reporting stages are conducted. In other words, you should 'trouble-shoot' the game before conducting it for the first time.

As in many types of group activity, at the end of the game group representatives report on what happened. Group observers may also be used and an observer will complete an observation form or checklist to report on the game, group dynamics or any other topic that has been assigned. Participants need time and an opportunity to think about and discuss the meaning of the game results and activities – what knowledge they have acquired, what future action they will take. In many games you might play a passive role during the actual activity, but then summarize at the end. You might comment on the group processes and results and, through discussion lead participants to learn from their game playing. Without this application stage, participant learning may stay in the game and not transfer in any significant way to real-life situations.

Participant presentations/demonstrations

Participant demonstrations are particularly important in skills training. In a course on how to use some new equipment, procedures or techniques, participant practice and demonstration are obviously required. In order to conduct these skills courses effectively, you need to:

- Provide a supportive, non-threatening, environment for participants to try out the skill. There should be an atmosphere of 'all colleagues together' and a sense of people helping each other to improve, rather than finding fault with each other.
- Allocate time for public and private feedback on the participant demonstrations. Public feedback can be given through oral comments and discussion. Private feedback can be provided through feedback forms that other participants and yourself fill in, and through private discussion between you and the participant. Videotaping each participant's demonstration and allowing him or her to look at it privately or together with you can be particularly helpful.
- Give a second chance. If participants feel that they have more than one chance at demonstrating a skill, they tend to feel much more relaxed and the emphasis in the first demonstration can be on improvement rather than evaluation. The first demonstration also gives the participant a chance to become comfortable with the demonstration task, the other participants and the atmosphere – most important of all, it gives a chance to make mistakes and learn from them.

Simulations and role-plays

Simulations and role-plays can provide people with practice in handling conflict and potentially stressful situations. They give participants an opportunity to try out the new communication or interpersonal skills they have learnt from a course. They also increase the job relevance of training and can provide the structured practice that is required to form new habits. Participants act out situations which they either face on the job or may face in the future. By doing this, they can examine their previous behaviour, assess and control their emotional involvement in a situation, and experiment with or rehearse new strategies. Role plays can either be provided for the participants or, more excitingly, produced by them. Here is an example of a role-play activity from a course for supervisors. The trainer and training materials recommend that the supervisor should take the following steps in conducting a corrective coaching session:

Steps in Corrective Coaching

1. State purpose of meeting and describe deficient performance
2. Get employee's agreement that a problem exists
3. Discuss alternative solutions
4. Mutually agree on action to correct the problem
5. Document the coaching meeting
6. Follow-up to assess results of the meeting.

Course participants are then asked to prepare for the following role play:

Think of an employee that works for you. Identify either one thing the employee is doing that he or she shouldn't be doing, or one thing the employee isn't doing and should be doing. Provide background details about the employee and the situation. Then prepare a corrective coaching plan following the coaching steps. Try to anticipate employee objections, particularly to the first two steps eg, refusal to admit that performance is deficient or that a problem exists. Be ready to role-play the corrective coaching session. Role-plays should take no longer than 15 minutes.

Participants are then given time to prepare for their role-play and draft their script. The very exercise of describing the problem situation or problem employee sometimes creates new insights and, combined with a focus on the coaching steps, may make participants feel confident for the first time of dealing with the situation. At the end of the preparation period, you might demonstrate and role-play with one of the participants. Alternatively, a mature and well-prepared participant might role-play a situation with another participant. It is important here to have a successful model which follows the corrective coaching steps. Participants can then pair up and conduct their own role-plays privately around the training room (perhaps with another participant observing and using the corrective coaching steps as a checklist) or publicly in front of you and the other participants.

Role-playing is time-consuming, particularly when each role-play is played out in front of the other participants. You need to stick closely to your time limit. When the time is up, you might move to the front of the room or make some other intervention to refocus attention and then go into the follow-up discussion.

Reverse role-plays can help participants gain an understanding of another person's viewpoint or see themselves as perceived by another person. In the corrective coaching situation the supervisor would become the subordinate and vice versa. Reverse role-plays are more likely to be successful with mature participants who are prepared, open to other perspectives, and unafraid of this experience. For immature participants the reverse role-play can be threatening and they may be afraid to *really* try to think themselves into the other person's skin.

Role-play feedback and discussion

Following a simulation or role-play, the discussion and observation comments should be constructive, non-threatening and informal so that participants feel relaxed after their experience. Discussion may well deal with feelings as much as it deals with the steps and the verbal content of the role-play. You might use as your opening question, 'How do you feel the role-play went?'. This open question can be followed by more precise questions focusing for example on how successfully a supervisor implemented the coaching steps. It is often useful here for you and the participants to be able to refer to the steps or procedures on a flipchart or posted up on the wall. Reference back to these steps or procedures helps imprint them in the participants' minds and illustrates their usefulness as guidelines.

In the corrective coaching role-play the opening question to the subordinate might be, 'How do you feel you were treated?'. Again more precise questions can follow focusing on the steps and how the subordinate responded to the supervisor's coaching. Other participants can then be allowed to comment. You should however moderate and control the comments of negative or highly critical participants. Comments like, 'Do not be too critical – it'll soon be your turn' can be effective in this situation.

Structured observation

Often in group activities, team games or role-plays the results are less important than the process by which the group arrived at its decisions, or the behaviour of the role-players. As mentioned earlier, you may be unable or reluctant to observe an activity, particularly when mature participants are involved. Indeed if the activity takes place in a team room, you may have no contact at all with the group process or role-play. In situations like this a participant is often used as an observer to watch the group process or the role-play. As a guide the observer is generally given an observation form, a checklist, or a series of questions to answer. For example, after the corrective coaching role-play the observer might answer the following questions (note how they follow the steps of the corrective coaching process):

1. Did the supervisor clearly state the purpose of the discussion?
2. Did the supervisor describe the unsatisfactory performance? Were concrete examples and data given?
3. Did the supervisor obtain agreement that a problem existed before discussing solutions? If yes, how did he or she do it?
4. Who developed most of the alternative solutions?
5. Did the supervisor and employee agree on a specific solution or action?
6. Did the supervisor set a follow-up date?
7. How do you think the employee and supervisor felt at the end of the discussion?

The observer's role is often a demanding one and a fairly mature and confident participant needs to be chosen, unless you are rotating every participant through the observation role. There is also a danger of the observer being treated by other participants as a spy, especially if at the reporting stage he or she reports there has been conflict in the group and they have been relatively unsuccessful in their task. In this situation you need to support the observer, but at the same time perhaps smooth ruffled participant feathers.

Participant questionnaires

As described in Chapter 3, participant questionnaires are mainly used to develop self-awareness and a readiness for change, either through training or other means of personal growth. We can see how useful questionnaires can be if we consider what is called the four-stage competence approach to training:

Stage 1: Unconscious incompetence – the participant is not aware that he or she needs or lacks the knowledge or skill required.
Stage 2: Conscious incompetence – the participant knows that he or she lacks the required knowledge or skill.
Stage 3: Conscious competence – the participant gains basic competence as a result of training and practice. He or she has to think about it though to perform to the required standard.
Stage 4: Unconscious competence (mastery) – the participant has used the knowledge or skill so often that he or she can now perform at or above the required standard almost without thinking.

One of the clearest examples of this process is learning to drive. As a child and in your early teens you do not feel the lack of driving knowledge or skill. This is Stage 1. However, as you grow older, you discover that you want to travel around more and your friends are learning to drive. This provides the motivation for you wanting to learn. This is Stage 2. Driving lessons and practice develop conscious competence so that when you pass the driving test you have a basic competence. At Stage 3 though, you generally still have to 'think' about your driving. Stage 4, unconscious competence, develops through the driving practice and experience that follow the driving test.

In a course on effective supervision there may be some people who are new to supervision, others who have been supervisors for some time, and even perhaps a few veteran supervisors who have been enrolled for a *refresher*. A good supervisory questionnaire will identify for each group of participants areas in which they can change and thus move them from Stage 1 – unconscious incompetence to Stage 2 – conscious incompetence.

There are a number of important steps you should take when using a participant questionnaire or instrument:

■ Create a non-threatening atmosphere by using the word *questionnaire* rather than *test*; reduce anxiety by making it clear that there are no 'right' answers. Let participants know that their bosses will not see their results and use humour whenever possible to defuse potential anxieties.

■ Show how the use of the questionnaire fits into the course and the training.
■ Encourage the participants to answer honestly and therefore promote greater self-learning. Point out that if they cheat, they are only cheating themselves of useful information.
■ Let people know that those who finish first will wait quietly for the rest. Encourage participants to take their time, to answer carefully and honestly.
■ Let participants complete the questionnaire, while you monitor and assist where necessary.
■ When everyone has completed, explain the scoring and give an example using one of your own responses to the questionnaire. Indeed some self-disclosure – how you have answered the questions – is helpful in reducing participant anxiety.
■ Don't force individuals to report their scores if they don't want to. When people do report on their results, avoid any appearance of diagnosing or labelling personalities. Make it clear that 'we' are all in a learning situation. Again disclosure of some of your own responses can be helpful here.
■ Allow sufficient time for assimilating and discussing the information obtained from completing the questionnaire.
■ Make it clear that different behaviours, opinions and perspectives are acceptable. Again everyone, including yourself, is in a learning situation.

Common situations

Situation: Participants are working on their second group exercise. The people who did all the work in the first group exercise are doing it all in the second. Several participants are sitting back chatting about their holiday plans.
Suggestions: This situation may indicate that the group size is too large for the task; the task is not properly formulated or challenging enough; or that you have allowed too much time. Adjust later group activities accordingly. To deal with the present situation, go to the group and suggest that the work might be shared more evenly. Indicate that the 'holiday planners' might have much to offer and that, in order to complete this task successfully, contributions are necessary from everyone. Try to be light and humorous in your intervention. You might change the composition of this group for the next group task.

Situation: Right from the opening introductions, it's clear that you have a know-it-all in this supervisors' course. He introduced himself as an experienced supervisor and is now dominating the discussion. In the middle of telling people what he thinks a supervisor should do, he gets up from his chair and goes to the flipchart to write up his ideas.
Suggestions: The 'know-it-all' is trying to take over. You should have discouraged him earlier by bringing in others as a counterweight and suggesting that he could

gain quite a lot by listening to them. You could also have pointed out in your introduction that a major aim in this training was to benefit from *everyone's* knowledge, experience and views. You have to deal with the present situation however. If you are sitting down for this discussion, now is the time to stand up in preparation for regaining control. Let the know-it-all write on the flipchart but encourage others to ask critical questions (participants are as likely as yourself to be fed up with this 'expert') and ask some searching questions yourself. Give him enough rope to hang himself or time to bore the others, and then intervene. Thank him for his contribution, say that it's time to move on, refer to the agenda and time constraints, and summarize the discussion. Move briskly to the next activity. Do not let the 'know-it-all' take over again – encourage others to make contributions and choose others as group leaders and reporters.

Situation: Four participants in the course are a higher status than the others. From the beginning these four participants have dominated and at times you feel the other participants are intimidated and reluctant to express their opinions.
Suggestions: Emphasize that you are all equal partners in the learning experience, regardless of differences in status back at the workplace. In your methods try to break away from large group work where the high status participants may dominate, to pair and small group work. Give as much opportunity as possible for the other participants to contribute. Make it clear to everyone that the all-important objective is effective learning. Status and other external factors should not be allowed to interfere with the achievement of that objective.

Situation: After a group activity the group representative is writing up findings on the flipchart. He is making a number of simple spelling mistakes. What should you do?
Suggestions: If you wait long enough, other participants might spot the mistakes and suggest corrections. Certainly it's better if the correction comes from others rather than yourself. If this does not happen, you might question one of the spellings. The writer might then admit he's never been a very good speller and you can joke about the vagaries of English spelling. Your main concern here however should be to limit embarrassment.

Situation: There are only five minutes left for the group work activity. You find that one group is still arguing about some basic points and hasn't come up with any action items or points for their report.
Suggestions: If you had monitored the group more carefully, this problem should not have arisen. Now you need to take a more directive approach, sit down and work with the group to produce their report. Lead the discussion and have the person who will be reporting start listing points on the flipchart. When the time comes for reporting let this group come in the middle. This gives them the benefit of the first presentation(s) and removes the pressure of being first or last to report.

Situation: Participants are preparing to role-play a job situation. One participant however is not doing any preparation at all. When you go over to her, she says she does not want to do the role-play.

Suggestions: Sit down with her and quietly ask why she does not want to participate. Be sympathetic but show that she is letting down the other participants and yourself by not taking part. Explain how this role-play will help her with her job. Try to pair her with a participant she gets on well with or, if necessary, offer to help her practise yourself.

Situation: You have presented some guidelines for supervisors on how to conduct a performance review interview. Participants are now role-playing interviews. During one interview however the two participants begin to quarrel bitterly.

Suggestions: Intervene with a good humoured comment and suggest that this is often what happens in review interviews. What participants are seeing now are the problems that can arise in these sessions. Get the role-players to identify the problems and the feelings they have and then ask other participants to comment. If participants don't feel comfortable enough yet to comment, make some observations yourself and relate these to the guidelines. This should help detach the role-players from the conflict and get everyone focused on the difficulties of performance review interviews. Encourage the role-players to continue and follow the guidelines.

Situation: Participants are involved in corrective coaching role-plays and following each role-play you and the other participants are providing feedback. During one role-play though, the 'supervisor' is too afraid to raise the problem and he never gets beyond the first step in the corrective coaching process. The role-play has just meandered to a stop.

Suggestions: Clearly point out to the 'supervisor' that he failed to identify the problem. Be understanding and sympathetic but you and the course will lose credibility if you do not point out what is obvious to everyone. Let the 'supervisor' start the role-play again.

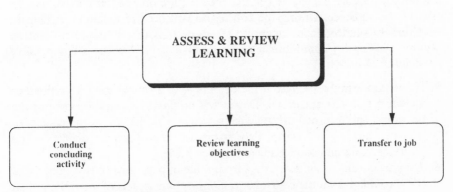

Figure 5.7 *Assess and review learning*

Assess and review learning

Every course, like every presentation, should have a beginning, a middle and an end. Trainers tend to spend a lot of time developing and conducting the introductory activities. A good opening makes you and the participants feel more comfortable and self-confident. The middle of the course is usually full of information and activities, and when participants get really involved in discussion or practice there is a tendency to let things 'run on'. The result is there is not much time for a conclusion. Both you and participants may therefore finish the course feeling slightly uncomfortable, that things were not fully completed or the training was not 'rounded off'.

At the end of a course therefore, make sure there is some time for a concluding activity. Although there is no hard-and-fast rule, about 5 per cent of the training time is usually sufficient. A concluding activity might be designed to:

■ Synthesize, bring together and apply, the knowledge or skills learned in the course.
■ Provide some feedback on, or evaluation of participant learning. For example, you might use a review quiz consisting of items that participants have developed.
■ Evaluate and discuss the performances or the products that are a result of the training eg, the demonstrations, the reports, the videotapes.
■ Link the training to on-the job applications.

People tend to 'turn off' and think about going home when they hear phrases like 'Now let's review what we've accomplished' or 'Now I'm going to summarize'. Participants however need a sense of the elements of the course being brought together, and they also need to consider how to continue learning through their jobs. Therefore it is much more effective to focus on the present or the future with comments like 'Let's pick out the key points we can use' or 'What things that you've learned are you going to use in your job?'. While a summary may aid retention, most are ineffective because they require only *passive listening* on the part of the audience. During the conclusion you need to maintain participant involvement – indeed involvement is perhaps even more important here because you are looking for commitment and transfer to job. Here are a few possible concluding activities:

■ If you conducted a pre-test at the beginning of a course, then it's natural to include a post-test at the end. Depending on the situation, this post-test can be scored and returned privately to participants at the end of the course, or later on during a follow-up. Participants can then compare their pre- and post-test scores and correct any errors they made.
■ Ask participants to jot down on a fresh piece of paper one or two points that come to mind from the course, or the one or two aspects of the training that were most helpful. Allow no more than five minutes, then elicit and list items

on the flipchart. As you write down the points, ask for clarification and amplification of points where necessary. Then ask for a show of hands on how many wrote down the same point.

■ Ask participants what they have learned that they can use on their first day back at work. What have they learned that will take more time to integrate into their work? Again these action items can be written down on the flipchart, clarified and amplified.

■ Similarly, in order to help participants prepare to apply what they have learned, you can suggest that they list problems or issues they hope to deal with more effectively after the course. Since individual situations always differ, they will need to be creative in their application of what they have learned.

■ Ask each participant or group of participants to make a brief presentation on something they have learned and how they will apply it.

■ In multiple-day courses participants are sometimes required to prepare an action plan for use back at work. This action plan can serve as a focus of discussion during the conclusion of the course and as a tool for a subsequent follow-up visit to the participant's worksite (see Chapter 6). In shorter courses participants might produce a short list of action items. In this way they can focus on what they have learned from the course and might apply when they go back to the job.

■ As an alternative to the action plan, learning journals are sometimes developed during multiple-day courses. At the beginning of the course, you might introduce the journal and explain how it can be used as a learning tool. Participants then note down key information, ideas they will use, reminders and their own creative ideas as they go through the course. At the end of each module or major activity you can provide time for participants to add to their journal. One major advantage of journal time is that this provides an opportunity for assimilation, reflection and perhaps personal goal-setting. You can also discuss the journals at the end of the course and at the subsequent follow-ups.

Common situations

Situation: Participants are being trained to make effective oral presentations. Their presentations are being videotaped and in order to complete the course, they have to meet the standards which have been explained earlier. One person's oral presentation clearly does not meet the standards – he did not spend enough time on preparing his material, he failed to follow the presentation model, and the presentation confused some of the participants. What should you do when you meet with him privately to view his videotape and discuss his performance?

Suggestions: Try to take an open, friendly and non-threatening attitude. Discuss with the participant the checklist and standards and other participants' oral and written feedback. Say that you will look at his videotape with these points in mind. Look at the videotape and stop at critical points. Ask the participant to comment on his preparation and presentation in relation to the presentation model. Then calmly and objectively look at specific techniques and whether the participant met the standards required. Lead him to admit he needs more help and further training in this area. If you allow someone to 'pass' the course who clearly did not deserve to pass, you will undermine the credibility of the training.

Situation: You are conducting a one-day course for a group of participants from the same department. The morning session has gone fairly smoothly but there are clearly people in the room who do not get on with each other. At the end of the afternoon session there's a general discussion of how the training can be applied back on the job. This suddenly breaks down into arguments and a clash of personalities. You feel things are getting out of control and you are angry that the course seems to be ending in a chaotic way.

Suggestions: When you are afraid that a course is getting out of control near the end, there is a natural tendency to retreat and 'get it over with quickly' – to cut the discussion short, quickly summarize and review the objectives. Do not do it. Clashes of personality are particularly common when participants come from the same department – they have had plenty of time to get to dislike or even hate each other (one of the disadvantages of working with an intact 'work group'). The other participants are probably used to these clashes though, are tired of the arguments and support your regaining control. Do not be stampeded into rushing the course to an end. You will feel dissatisfied and many of the participants will feel cheated of a satisfactory closing.

Co-training

It is often beneficial to have two trainers conduct particularly demanding or multiple-day courses. Indeed co-training improves almost any training session and research has shown that trainers learn most effectively from co-training and working with each other. Co-training helps trainers by:

■ Improving their training skills. In particular, trainers can learn a great deal through their joint preparation and rehearsal for a course. They can test ideas on one another and reassess direction and strategy not only during the course preparation, but while conducting the course itself.

■ Adding to the energy trainers bring to their training. Trainers working by themselves have to manage many different tasks at the same time – pushing on and keeping track of the objectives and content, managing activities and time, and continuously monitoring participant reactions. The amount of concentration required and the potential stress can be exhausting. In co-training however, neither person is 'on all the time' and can conserve personal energy. While one speaks, the other can perform important functions such as assessing participant reactions and needs and planning adjustments in the course. Just as the exchanges between co-presenters on TV news programmes contribute

to the liveliness and interest of the programme, so the exchanges between co-trainers can make sessions more dynamic and stimulating.
■ Allowing each trainer to come to the other's rescue when necessary. One of the trainer's greatest fears is going blank in the middle of a presentation or being unable to answer an important question. But when one trainer goes blank, gets off track, or is unable to answer a question, the partner can come to the rescue.

If co-training benefited only the trainers, it would be difficult to justify the costs. Co-training however also benefits participants by:

■ Providing a variety of training styles and increased variety of presentation, voice, pace, tone, etc.
■ Increasing the diversity, variety and richness of the course experience. When I and my usual co-trainer present, participants get the benefit of more than 40 years training experience, two different cultural backgrounds (Western and Middle-Eastern), and perspectives from three languages – English, French and Arabic.
■ Closer monitoring, and from this, more attention to individual needs and interests. In courses where participants are videotaped, one trainer can do the videotaping and provide private feedback, while the other trainer continues to conduct the course.
■ Increasing participant attention. Participants focus on both trainers individually and the interaction between them.

The following techniques are often used in co-training:

Duet. The two trainers can balance 'the stage' with one standing on the right, the other on the left. They cue each other through eye contact to indicate 'I want to add something', glances at the watch to indicate time concerns, hand gestures, voice and intonation.

Turn-taking. The two trainers take turns at presenting. It works well where there is a lot of presentation material in a course or there is new material that one or both presenters have not yet fully assimilated.

Speak-and-add. One leads, the other supports. The support may add lightness or humour, if the lead trainer gets too heavy or dry. The support can bring the lead back to the central theme if there is a digression, or intervene in a discussion to bring things back on course. *Speak-and-add* lets co-trainers capitalize on their different perspectives and experiences.

Speak-and-record. While the lead trainer elicits participant responses, the support can record the responses on the flipchart. He or she therefore acts as the session's recorder. Important points here are that:

■ the lead trainer must monitor the accuracy and speed with which the support trainer records. Either the lead trainer or the support can slow the process

down by asking participants to clarify their responses, requesting examples and comments from other participants, or summarizing the points made so far;
- the support must summarize ideas quickly without distorting concepts or vocabulary. This requires good writing skills;
- the support must remain a neutral recorder, not express opinions or evaluate the points, and only speak when requesting clarification. He or she has the responsibility of providing a group record, one that is acceptable to all and that may be returned to later.

Other points and techniques to note in co-training are that co-trainers should:

- Be in agreement that the overriding goal is to increase participant learning. Each trainer has a responsibility to support and make the other look good. They should be prepared to do whatever it takes to achieve the desired outcome, whether that means interrupting each other, making photocopies, arranging the furniture, or breaking the ice with participants before the session begins.
- Model rapt attention to each other's words as if they are hearing them for the first time. They should also be prepared to change roles at times to add variety.
- Be ready to adjust the planned content and activities of the course to meet the requirements of each audience and setting.
- Have ongoing permission to monitor and intervene when necessary. However, once the support trainer signals that time is running out, he or she should leave the lead trainer alone. Co-trainers need to trust each other to make the appropriate adjustments.
- Discuss what worked, what did not, and why after each session. Good co-trainers apply this information when they plan for future sessions.

Not every session will go perfectly but co-training can be an effective and rewarding way to train. It conveys the instructional material but it goes deeper too. Co-training communicates collaboration and peer learning, and when we co-train we signal that we are all learners.

Project Action Items: Assess your own performance

Trainers learn best from observing other trainers and getting feedback from them. You can learn from:

- conducting a dry-run in front of your colleagues
- having a colleague videotape your presentation
- asking your colleagues for general suggestions or more specifically to complete a feedback form or checklist like the one below.

Note that in this feedback form it is possible to put a check mark in both the 'good' and 'needs work' boxes. For example, there might be some good visuals and some that need improvement. Your colleague(s) may use a question mark (?) if an activity should appear but doesn't, and N/A for not applicable. In the comments/suggestions section, strengths as well as suggestions for improvement should be noted.

TRAINING FEEDBACK FORM
Trainer's name: _____
Training objective as stated: _____
_____
_____

PERFORMANCE	GOOD	NEEDS WORK	COMMENTS/ SUGGESTIONS
1. Stated session objective(s) clearly, including employee action(s), any conditions, and the standard(s) required			
2. Explained how the objective(s) related to employee jobs and interests – What's In It For Me			
3. Elicited employee's previous knowledge/experience related to training topic			
4. Explained main points of the training session clearly and in logical sequence			
5. Used visual aids – handouts/flipchart/ transparencies/ slides/video – effectively to highlight main points			

PERFORMANCE	GOOD	NEEDS WORK	COMMENTS/ SUGGESTIONS
6. Used questions to involve employees and check understanding			
7. Encouraged employees' own questions/comments			
8. Used appropriate delivery skills: • Interest/enthusiasm shown • Eye contact – all employees • Gestures and movement – natural • Voice – loud enough, pace and tone vary, pauses used • Language – understandable, no jargon or slang			
9. Provided enough time to apply/practice new information			
10. Used an evaluation tool and/or reviewed the session with employees			

Presentation strengths: _____

_____

_____

_____

_____

Additional comments/suggestions: _____

_____

_____

_____

_____

6

How to evaluate training effectiveness and job performance

This chapter discusses the reasons for and the methods available for following-up on and evaluating the effectiveness of training. We will discuss five different levels of evaluation: how each level of evaluation is conducted, its benefits and limitations. In particular, we will consider the relatively new areas of workplace assessment and how to evaluate training's impact on the organization.

Evaluation is one aspect of training whose time has come – in some cases with a vengeance. Historically, evaluation has tended to be low on the list of priorities for training departments. In the past the main struggle was to develop and conduct training programmes that fitted the needs of the organization and its employees. Now with training programmes being developed and implemented on a larger scale than ever before, managements are looking for a return on their investment. Increasingly trainers are required to evaluate their programmes and justify their organization's expenditure on training.

Evaluation has traditionally been placed at the end of the training cycle and, like most things that are placed at the end of a long and sometimes difficult process, it has tended to be skimped or neglected in favour of the next project. Over recent years, however, with the development of workplace assessment, job certification and an increased emphasis on results, more attention is being directed to evaluation. Particularly in a period when rationalization and cost-effectiveness are the order of the day, management requires hard facts about the effectiveness of training, evidence of past success and value for money. Commenting on this situation, Kenneth R Robinson (1988) writes:

The biggest problem it [training] faces in this age of competition for resources is that in many key areas it is extremely difficult to measure the effects of training in absolute terms. Whilst in a production environment it is fairly straightforward to assess output, quality, scrap etc, the measurement of the effectiveness of, for example, management training is much less practicable since so many other dynamic factors can mask the results....This lack of a positive means of evaluation leaves many managers in the position where they see training as a greater financial risk than other options for investment of the organization's stretched financial resources. This is disquieting because such decisions are taken at the very time that an investment in training could help an organization along the road to greater efficiency and effectiveness and in some cases survival. One of the highest priorities for training departments today is to find a means of evaluating training activities which will convince their managements of the contribution that training can make to the success of the business.

One reason why the evaluation of training has become so important is the rise in training costs. In 1993 US companies spent more than $48 billion on employee training (*Training* magazine, October 1992). Yet few companies can show that their training expenditure results in observable measurable changes on the job. Indeed, studies in the US show that only about 15 per cent of companies measure the transfer of training – employees' application of the knowledge and skills gained through training.

Attitudes to evaluation

We can identify three main attitudes to the role of evaluation in training. First there is the view that training, like education, is generally a good thing and therefore evaluation is not really necessary. Managers and trainers who hold this view are not very definite about the purposes of training and tend to see evaluation in rather subjective and vague terms – 'They enjoyed the course' or 'He/she seems to have learned something'. The bottom line here though is that in a period of recession people with this viewpoint see training as a luxury that can be cut and then perhaps 'picked up again later' when business improves.

A second, and still fairly common view, is that the development and delivery of courses to large numbers of employees is the most important thing. At best, this attitude has an air of missionary zeal and idealism; at worst, it treats training as a 'numbers game'. Managers and training staff with this point of view tend to accept evaluation as a necessary evil but consider that time spent on evaluation is wasted training time. In addition, trainers with this point of view sometimes see evaluation as just another way for the administrators to criticize the trainers who are doing the 'real work of training all these people'.

Finally, there is the view that evaluation is necessary and can improve the effectiveness of instruction and materials and ensure that training transfers to the job. Managers and trainers holding this view believe that evaluation can provide solid support and justification for quality training. They use evaluation, measurements of *training transfer* and evidence of business results to provide data justifying training costs.

As someone who has held all three views at different times, I now adhere to the virtuous third. Indeed this view has become the only viable one for training staff. Management support is unlikely if trainers ignore the fact that the effectiveness of training has to be demonstrated and proved.

The highest priority therefore is to devise evaluation procedures and instruments which will provide evidence to management of training's contribution to business success. If satisfactory methods of evaluating training can be found, there are benefits for everyone. The organization is better equipped to meet its manpower requirements, management's decision to invest money in training is justified, and trainers not only still have a job to do but feel more confident and satisfied with what they are doing.

Before we can determine the methods or tools of evaluation though, we need to identify the purposes of our evaluation.

Purposes of evaluation

Evaluation may be seen as having three main purposes. First, the improvement of training programmes. One of the most common reasons for evaluation is to determine the effectiveness of training so that future programmes can be improved. Basically, evaluation that does not lead to improved practice is sterile. Evaluation provides information that can be used in the development of new courses, the revision of existing courses, or to eliminate inappropriate or ineffective training. This type of evaluation to improve the quality of training programmes is often known as *formative evaluation*.

Second, the assessment of the value of training to participants. This involves the evaluation of improvements in participants' job performance This type of evaluation takes place some time after an employee has completed a training programme and is often known as *summative evaluation*.

Third, the assessment of the value of training to participants' organizations. This involves a comparison between these financial benefits and the costs involved – what is known as the *return on investment (ROI)*. Some companies are now treating training as an investment rather than a cost. However, as with any kind of new investment, they require sound business reasons to justify new training programmes and expenditure. Indeed only when training can show a business impact and significant results will it be able to move from the business cost column to the investment column.

These three purposes of evaluation are reflected in five different levels and methods of evaluation.

Levels of evaluation

We can identify five different levels of evaluation. These relate to:

1. Training programme development

2. Participant reactions
3. Participant learning
4. Participant job performance
5. Business impact.

Let us look at these levels in more detail.

Level 1: Training programme development

This level involves you in conducting continuous evaluation during the development of training. Rather than treating evaluation as a discrete step at the end of the training cycle, you treat it as an integral part of training programme development. This is *formative evaluation*, the on-going evaluation which you conduct as you are in the process of actually developing a course. In this way evaluation is linked to the needs assessment, the development of objectives and the training activities.

How it's done
In meetings, discussions and rehearsals of the course activities, trainers are involved in informal evaluation throughout the development process. This results in many on-the-spot improvements. In Chapter 3 we discussed the importance of the *dry-run* as an evaluation checkpoint or a tool for decision-making. As a result of the dry-run, it is often necessary to make significant revisions to a training programme. After the pilot presentation also, you will generally make revisions based on your own experience in conducting the programme and participant feedback collected through forms like the one shown in Figure 6.1.

Benefits
Evaluation is intimately connected with the pre-training needs survey and the establishment of objectives. Consciousness of evaluation requirements obliges you to focus more precisely on identifying staff needs and training objectives when developing the programme. The more precise the objectives, the more precisely can training be evaluated; evaluation forces you to concentrate on achieving the objectives of the training programme

Through the dry-run and the pilot presentation, you can systematically improve the training before it's finally presented to participants.

Limitations
A training course may be very attractive and responses from trainers and the first participants may be very encouraging. The effectiveness of the training however can not be judged on the responses to the dry-run or pilot presentation.

Level 2: Participant reactions

Did participants like the course? This level of evaluation involves the collection

Directions: Now that you have completed this training course we would like to know your thoughts about the course as a whole. Please take a few minutes to answer the following questions.

I. COURSE CONTENT: Please indicate the appropriate comment.

TOPIC	Very useful	Useful	Somewhat useful	Not useful

Which session did you find most useful?

Why? _____

Which session did you find least useful?_____

Why? _____

What topics, if any, should be added to the course? _____

_____

2. COURSE PRESENTATION: Please indicate the appropriate comment.

TOPIC	Very Effective	Effective	Somewhat effective	Ineffective presentation

Which session was most effectively presented?

Why? _____

Which session was least effectively presented?_____

Why? _____

3. COURSE TIMING: Please indicate whether the following topics needed more time, less time, or the time allocated was just right.

TOPIC	More time	Time right	Less time

This is an x-day course. Please indicate by a check mark whether the course is:

Too short   About right in length   Too long

5. COMMENTS/SUGGESTIONS FOR IMPROVEMENT:

_____

_____

Thank you for taking the time to complete this feedback form.

                                    Name: _____(Optional)

Figure 6.1 *Course feedback form*

TRAINING COURSE EVALUATION
Course Title: _____
Date: _____ Location:_____
Course Leader(s): _____

Please evaluate the course in the following areas by checking the appropriate rating: **E** for Excellent, **VG** for Very Good, **G** for Good, **F** for Fair, **P** for Poor

STATEMENT	E	VG	G	F	P
1. Course relevance and usefulness in job					
2. Participation and involvement					
3. Practical discussion and exercises					
4. Sufficient time for course activities					
5. Overall effectiveness of course leader(s)					
6. Overall effectiveness of course					
7.					
8.					

Write in the spaces above other statements you want feedback on.

Identify three things you learned from the course:

1. _____
2. _____
3. _____

Explain how you will apply these three things on the job:

1. _____
2. _____
3. _____

Was this course at the right time in your job and career? Should you have taken it sooner or later?

_____
_____

Additional comments/suggestions:

_____
_____
_____

Would you recommend this programme to others? Yes( ) No( )

Employee signature (optional): _____ Date: _____

Figure 6.2 *Training course evaluation*

and assessment of participants' reactions through evaluation or feedback forms. These forms are usually distributed and completed at the end of a course and consist of questions or statements with some kind of numerical or descriptive rating scale, as shown in the course evaluation form in Figure 6.2. Generally such forms are developed by the training department or trainer(s) to be used for all courses. You might develop customized forms, however, to obtain specific information on new or special courses.

How it's done

Here are a few suggestions about how you might develop your own course feedback form. Many of the suggestions made earlier in Chapter 2 about the development of questionnaires also apply to the development of feedback forms.

■ Try to involve other trainers and participants in the design of the form and gain the value of other perspectives and ideas.
■ Before developing your form, decide what you want to know. Indeed your form will indicate those aspects of the training to which you attach most importance. One thing to avoid here is too many questions asking for views on the trainer's effectiveness – this indicates that a course is trainer-centred rather than learning-centred. Indeed, the focus should not be on the trainer's popularity but on the effectiveness of the learning experience. In Figure 6.2 most of the questions require participants to relate the course and what they learned to their jobs.
■ Group the questions or items on the form. Do not force participants to switch from one topic to another and back again. You might have a few questions on the effectiveness of the course and the trainer, several questions on the applicability of training to the job, etc.
■ Ensure that you can convert some of the participant reactions into a numerical rating for tabulating and quantifying reactions. When you conduct a large number of courses, computer scoring becomes a key consideration.
■ By using a standardized form you can compare your courses in particular areas eg, job relevance.
■ As well as closed questions or statements, provide an opportunity and sufficient space for participant comments and suggestions. These responses are often more valuable than those to the 'rating scale' items.
■ Use unsigned feedback forms. If you oblige participants to identify themselves, you are likely to get overly positive feedback. This may look good in the eyes of your management, but it will not help identify a weak course or help you revise it.
■ Keep the form simple and ensure that it only takes a short time to complete.
■ Use the feedback form several times before finalizing it. Then make the form look as professional as possible and print it.

Benefits

Feedback forms can provide:

■ An opportunity for participants to review their learning and give their views and suggestions on the training. Completing the course feedback form also provides participants with a sense of 'closure' to the course.

■ A relatively cheap and easy method of evaluation. The form provides a familiar format for responses and should be easy for participants to complete. If you give out the forms near the end of the course, you can ensure a 100 per cent return rate.

■ Feedback to individual trainers on specific courses. The responses to a feedback form distributed and collected at the end of a course are immediate and can indicate to you those parts of the course which are in urgent need of attention.

■ Feedback to the training supervisor and staff on the whole programme. Participant responses can help with the 'steering' of a training programme, help you decide what direction to take and what to do next in the development or revision of training.

■ Feedback to management on staff training. The data obtained from feedback forms can be easily quantified and presented to management on a regular basis. In an important sense the forms provide a means of measuring customer satisfaction with training.

■ Material for publicity and marketing purposes. You might quote comments made by participants in the form's suggestions or comments section when you next advertise a training course.

Limitations

The feedback form may make trainers anxious and focus more on 'popularity' and whether everybody liked them, rather than on participant learning. The trainer who challenges participants or demands more may receive lower ratings than an easy-going 'entertainer'.

Reaction evaluations may provide useful information for improving courses, but they do not indicate how training will affect job performance or organizational results. It seems logical that participants who enjoy a course are more likely to benefit from it. However, there may be little correlation between how participants feel about a course and what they learned or, more critically what they will do as a result of it. The popularity of a course or a trainer gives no assurance that learning has taken place or that participants will change because of the course.

Forms distributed at the end of a course are usually completed in a hurry and this often results in participants producing superficial *smile sheets*. Some participants also may not feel in a position to make a reasoned assessment of the course when lots of ideas are still buzzing around in their heads.

In order to avoid smile sheets, some trainers prefer to send out feedback forms several weeks after a course. The theory is that participants will have had time to consider the value of the training and be able to comment more realistically on its effects and relevance. In practice however, a large number of forms may not be completed or returned and the trainer is forced to spend a lot of time progress-chasing. This is annoying not only for the trainer, but for the people being chased.

Another way to avoid the smile sheet and 'popularity contest' dangers of feedback forms is for the training supervisor or another qualified person to attend the course and fill out an evaluation form independent of the group's reactions. Using the supervisor's evaluation form together with that of participants may well give the best indication of the effectiveness of a course.

Level 3: Participant learning

This involves an evaluation of the knowledge and skills participants have gained through the course. Did they meet the objectives of the course? Particularly in courses where skills are being taught, you should plan systematic evaluation to measure participant learning and whether the course objectives were met. This evaluation of learning is however more difficult and time-consuming than the evaluation of participant reactions and responses.

How it's done

Quizzes or tests can be used to assess the knowledge that participants have gained. In some training programmes a pre- and post-test approach is used to evaluate the knowledge gained through a course and to set up a self-correcting training system. Whatever the situation however, a quiz or test should relate directly to the course objectives, be representative of the training, and allow learners to demonstrate their new knowledge. In most cases we are not testing participants' writing skills or their ability to produce a long essay. Objective questions like those shown in Figure 6.3 therefore tend to be used. These are more comprehensive, can be completed more quickly and are easier to score than long answer tests. Objective questions also not only serve to check participant's understanding, but can be used for review purposes and to stimulate discussion.

Performance tests require participants physically to demonstrate skills or their application of knowledge. You must however ensure that the test covers the key requirements of skill performance that have been specified during the training. For example, in a demonstration techniques course the trainer and other participants might comment on the participant's performance by using a feedback form such as Figure 6.4.

Supervisory and management training courses often involve performance testing in the form of role-plays and skills practice exercises. For example, participants may be asked to demonstrate problem-solving or communication skills through a simulation. This again may be evaluated by the other participants and the trainer.

Another way of finding out how much participants have learned is through evaluation of what they have produced – a word-processed letter, a written report, a videotape. Even when the primary objectives of a training programme involve

Objective testing

True-false questions

Indicate whether the following statements are true or false:

1. Formative evaluation is concerned with assessing the importance of training to the company.   *True/False*
2. Summative evaluation is concerned with assessing improvements in job performance.   *True/False*

Multiple-choice questions

Indicate the best answer by circling the number:

The most common type of training evaluation is of:

1. Job performance   2. Participant reactions
3. Organizational impact   4. Participant learning

Matching item questions

For each item, write a number to indicate that the statement applies to:

       1. Norm-referenced assessment
       2. Criterion-referenced assessment

_____ Assessment is based on mastery
_____ Assessment usually involves percentages or letter grades
_____ Assessment is used for educational selection

Completion questions

Complete the following sentences:

1. For the workplace assessor relevant evidence might include   _____
   _____
2. The workplace assessor uses questions to   _____
3. Feedback should be _____ and _____ to be effective.

Rank-order questions

Rank the following levels of evaluation in order of importance to your training programme. Use 1 to indicate the most important and 5 the least important level:

_____ Training programme development   _____ Participant learning

_____ Participant reactions   _____ Job performance

_____ Organizational impact

Figure 6.3 *Objective questions*

Demonstration feedback form

Trainer's Name : _____

Directions : Check(✔) the performances when they occur.

PERFORMANCES	CHECK	COMMENTS
1. Trainer stated demonstration objective(s)/showed end-product		
2. Trainer stimulated audience's interest		
3. Trainer explained and showed the steps		
4. Trainer avoided mirror image in his demonstration		
5. Trainer made sure everyone could see the demonstration		
6. Trainer asked questions to increase/ check understanding.		
7. Trainees explained and trainer showed the steps		
8. Trainees explained and showed the steps		
9. Trainer involved every trainee in the activity		
10. Trainer provided feedback to trainees.		
11. Trainer provided practice time		
12. Trainer evaluated trainee performance/end product		

STRENGTHS	SUGGESTIONS

Figure 6.4 *Demonstration techniques feedback form*

Learning journal

Course:_____

Participant Name: _____ Date: _____

```
┌──────────────────────────────────────────────────┐
│                 THINGS TO DISCUSS                   │
│                                                     │
│                                                     │
│                                                     │
│                                                     │
│                                                     │
└──────────────────────────────────────────────────┘
```

```
┌──────────────────────────────────────────────────┐
│                THINGS TO THINK ABOUT                │
│                                                     │
│                                                     │
│                                                     │
│                                                     │
│                                                     │
└──────────────────────────────────────────────────┘
```

```
┌──────────────────────────────────────────────────┐
│                   THINGS TO DO                      │
│                                                     │
│                                                     │
│                                                     │
│                                                     │
└──────────────────────────────────────────────────┘
```

Figure 6.5 *Daily Learning Journal*

increased knowledge and skills, changes in attitudes are often required. Such changes though are more difficult to measure objectively than increases in knowledge or skill. You can, however, use information gained from participant questionnaires, role-plays, or learning journals (see Figure 6.5) to assess any changes in participant attitudes. For a performance test to be effective you need to:

■ Plan the test thoroughly – the timing, preparation of participants, collection of materials and tools, evaluation of the results.
■ Make the test representative of the course. The test should allow participants to demonstrate as many skills as possible that are taught in the course. This

strategy increases the validity of the test and makes it more meaningful to participants.

■ Give thorough and consistent instructions. If possible, the test should be demonstrated by the trainer so that participants see how the skill is practised. Charts, diagrams, blueprints and other supporting information should be provided if they are normally provided in the work setting.

■ Develop procedures for effective evaluation. Establish predetermined standards so that participants know in advance what has to be accomplished to be considered satisfactory and acceptable for the test. Performance checklists are often useful here.

■ Use more than one assessor to improve the test's objectivity.

Benefits

When participants know that the course involves evaluation activities and that they will be held accountable for learning, they tend to pay more attention and take a more serious attitude.

Quizzes and performance tests provide more relevant information on the effectiveness of a course than participant reaction forms. During the course you can assess the effectiveness of a participant's demonstration, performance in a role-play, or the quality of the product that a participant or group of participants produce.

Limitations

It is more difficult to assess performance and learning than to assess and tabulate reactions recorded on feedback forms. As a result, performance evaluation is a more expensive means of evaluation. In particular, you need more development and testing time for the production of evaluation instruments than for the development of a feedback form.

Evaluation activities can take up a lot of time in a course. If each participant has to do a performance test, this puts a limit on the number of participants you can accept. For example, if each participant has to make a 15 minute presentation and this is followed by a feedback discussion of 15 minutes, then with only six participants the evaluation activity will take at least three hours. If you increase the number of participants in such courses, you need to increase the number of trainers.

There is always a danger of over-subjectivity in assessing participant performance. Evaluation tools ie, forms and procedures, need to be used to make your assessment more objective and reliable. Two trainers may also need to be assigned to a performance-based course to improve the 'objectivity' of assessment.

Training takes place in artificial conditions which cannot accurately reflect the reality of the job situation. How a participant performs in a course does not tell you how well he or she will perform on the job and whether learning will be applied. You may try to simulate the job atmosphere by developing exercises from real life, by role-plays, simulations and case studies, yet some participants will still say or think, 'But this isn't like it is in real life!'. Evaluation conducted as part of the course, however, does indicate participants' level of competence and what they can do in a controlled situation.

Some people are more accustomed to adapting theory and knowledge to constantly varying situations and can 'perform' well in front of others in demonstrations, presentations, role-plays, etc. A good performance in a training course, however, does not guarantee a good performance on the job. Conversely some participants may feel threatened by the evaluation activities and may perform badly due to anxiety.

Level 4: Participant job performance

Here we are asking 'Can participants apply the knowledge and skills they have learned?' This is *summative evaluation*. Certainly you can not tell how effective training is just by looking at participants in the training room. You can only judge effectiveness when you see how the training has been understood and is used under the everyday conditions of the job. Follow-up visits and observations at the job site are therefore a must for trainers. They not only provide feedback on the effectiveness of training and support to participants trying to apply their learning, but can also increase management support and involvement in training. Such support and involvement is critical if employees are going to implement what they have learned and to overcome potential obstacles in the work environment.

Traditionally trainers have concentrated on the development and delivery of training programmes. A strong correlation exists however between training transfer and the quality and amount of managerial support. Trainers therefore need to focus more on involving managers and seeing that they support training on the job. Here is a simple formula which highlights the importance of management involvement in training.

Effectiveness of Training x Client Involvement = Training Results
$$ET \times CI = TR$$

You could, for example, have 10 for effectiveness (a good programme, participants involved, etc.) but if there is only a 2 for client involvement (little or no involvement and commitment from the department), the results will be small:

$$10 \times 2 = 20$$

If however you spend more time on increasing client involvement, you will obtain greater results than if you spend that time on making minor improvements in training:

$$ET \times CI = TR$$
$$8 \times 5 = 40$$

In other words, a relatively small improvement in the client's commitment will double the impact. The lesson of this is that to increase the effectiveness of training, trainers need to work with the departments and ensure that managers are involved and committed to the training of their staff. This is one of the main reasons for follow-up and evaluation of job behaviour.

How it's done

When there is going to be follow-up at the job-site, inform participants, preferably at the beginning of the course, and tell them who will conduct the follow-up and how. Such follow-ups may be conducted by the participant's manager or supervisor, the trainer or perhaps some external evaluator. Whoever does the follow-up should have some kind of plan and preferably some observation tools and training in follow-up.

Follow-up by the manager or supervisor. One of the simplest and most effective means of follow-up consists of a meeting between the employee and his or her manager or supervisor. The meeting should focus on what the employee has learned and how he or she is going to apply it to the job. Figure 6.6 was developed in order to provide a structure for such a meeting. This type of review should be a regular activity after each course an employee attends

A more demanding means of follow-up involves managers attending a briefing on the training course before their staff attend. For example, before a course on supervision you might brief participants' managers so that they know what their supervisors should learn from the course. Following the course, a questionnaire can be distributed to managers asking them about their supervisors' post-training performance. This questionnaire would oblige managers to observe their staff and assess performance in the specific areas dealt with in the supervisory training. The questionnaire could then be used at a meeting between the manager and supervisor and used as input for the performance review process.

Follow-up by the trainer or external evaluator. When you or an external evaluator follow-up at the job-site this can involve:

■ Discussions or interviews with the supervisor and participant.
■ Assessment of project work, an action plan, or learning journal completed by the participant.
■ Job observation or workplace assessment.

Discussion or interviews

Just as in the needs survey, you must prepare for and structure any follow-up discussions or interviews to make the most of them. Figure 6.6. lists some of the questions you might use at a follow-up meeting with either a supervisor or participant. The comments under each question provide some explanation or suggestions you might follow.

Assessment of project work, action plan, or learning journal

One way to establish a direct link between training and the workplace is to give participants a project to complete when they return to their jobs. Each project

Follow-up meeting outline

Explain the purpose of your follow-up visit. Try to maintain an informal relaxed style and put the supervisor or participant at ease.

Could you tell me about your/the participant's work situation at the moment? Try to establish the job situation and context eg, staffing and workload, current projects, points of concern, etc.

What do you think you/your staff member learned from the course? Encourage the supervisor or participant to identify specific information or skills that were learned.

Which part of the course did you/your staff member find most helpful or relevant? Review the different topics or parts of the course. You may need to refresh the participant's memory here.

Which part of the course seemed least helpful/least relevant? Indicate by your voice and attitude that you're looking for suggestions and that you're interested in improving the training programme.

Refer to any action plan or action items that the participant produced during the course. Discuss progress on the plan or items.

What problems have you/your staff member encountered in putting the ideas from the course into practice? Discuss any obstacles which are present in the work environment and which might prevent the participant implementing what he or she has learned.

What solutions have you adopted? Discuss possible solutions. The solutions adopted by one person may be of use to others in a similar situation.

What additional training or help would be useful? Provide some information here on what other training courses and services are available.

What additional training or help do others, eg, new staff, need? Encourage the supervisor or participant to make suggestions. If the discussion is with a supervisor he or she will often speak about enrolling other employees in training sessions.

Figure 6.6 *Sample follow-up meeting outline*

should form part of the participant's normal work, employ principles or techniques covered in the training, and require a certain amount of research in the job. Discussion of this project during a follow-up can establish how effective learning has been and evaluation of the project will indicate to you whether or not further training is necessary.

Another means of encouraging the transfer of training is for you to make *action planning* an integral part of the course. On the action plan form participants should record their proposed actions, the timing and the names or positions of the people involved. By creating such plans, people make contracts with themselves to implement the skills they have learned, thus increasing the likelihood that transfer will occur. During a follow-up visit the action plan can provide a focus of discussion with participants and their supervisors.

A learning journal, such as the one shown in Figure 6.5 can also be used in the same way with participants noting down how they are trying to apply their learning to the job and what the results are.

An alternative to the on-site follow-up visit is to split a training course into two parts separated by a period of one or more weeks. The project, action plan, or learning journal is developed in the first part of the course, completed on the job during the intervening period, and presented for evaluation at an individual follow-up or *call-back* session. At this session you can discuss with each participant the transfer of learning to the job and assess their project, action plan or learning journal.

One important benefit of projects and action planning is that participants can make plans and commitments to follow-up on ideas while they are still fresh in their minds. If this is not done, learning may well be forgotten and the benefits of training lost.

Job observation or workplace assessment

Job observation or workplace assessment may be conducted by the trainer, the employee's supervisor or an external evaluator. Over the past few years the development of competence-based training and assessment programmes like those for the British National Vocational Qualifications have led to an increased emphasis on workplace assessment or evaluation. The success of such job certification systems depends upon having reliable, consistent and constructive workplace assessment.

When people observe they tend to use themselves and what they think of as *their* performance as standards. To avoid this kind of subjectivity observers need to use a consistent procedure and structured observation forms; these can guide the observation, provide usable feedback for the employee and document and justify any decisions on certification. Detailed guidelines for conducting workplace assessment are listed in Figure 6.7 but here are some additional points and examples to consider.

Workplace assessor guidelines

If one of the steps is not applicable, mark N/A in the box.

Preparation

Review the candidate's training for the task which is to be evaluated
Inform the candidate of the date and the relevant element/unit for assessement
Check that the candidate has access to all materials, equipment, etc. required to complete the task
Ensure that you can explain clearly what the candidate needs to demonstrate, show knowledge of and understand, for you to enter 'competency'
Prepare questions on the task/procedure to be demonstrated
Identify any high risk or criterion steps listed in the task/procedure checklist

Briefing

Write down the candidate's name and employee number
Put the candidate at ease before the assessment begins
State the relevant topic/element/module clearly. Highlight safety factors
Discuss candidate's training, check prior knowledge and/or relevant evidence
Outline the assessment procedure. Encourage questions to ensure the candidate understands your role and what he or she is expected to do

Assessment Procedure

Remain as unobtrusive as possible. Do not help or hinder during the assessment (verbally or physically)
Administer pre-set simulations and tests as required
Give clear and specific guidelines on the task eg, I want you to do X in the specified manner and you have X minutes to do it
Keep your assessment to the performance criteria specified in the assessment tool
Ensure your questions are clear and concise. Avoid leading questions
Check candidate's competence thoroughly – performance, understanding and knowledge
Check the time accurately if speed is being evaluated
Record your assessment and comments as soon as possible during the assessment. Important points can be forgotten if left until later

Feedback

Take the candidate to a quiet area and talk privately
Give positive, specific and constructive feedback on the assessment. Highlight any areas for improvement or retraining
State clearly whether further evidence is required or retraining/reassessment is necessary. Giving a clear decision is important

Records

Write comments on the candidate's performance on a record sheet. Show these to the candidate
Fill in supplementary information if it is required and is available
If the candidate has not met the standards, arrange a retraining and reassessment date. Record this information on the appropriate sheets

Figure 6.7 *Workplace assessor guidelines*

Briefing
Here is a sample dialogue:

Assessor: Hello Joe. Please take a seat and make yourself comfortable. As you know the purpose of this session is for me to assess you on task X. This is part of the Training and Assessment unit X. How have you found your training? You remember I asked you to bring along some examples of X. Have you got these with you? Now a brief explanation of my role. I will stay in the background and make notes while you complete the task. I will ask a few questions but it would be helpful if you explained what you were doing as you went along, mentioning any important points. At the end of the session I will ask you some more questions. I will then give you feedback on your performance and a clear decision. At that stage we can review progress and you will have the opportunity to ask any questions. Have you any questions on the assessment process before we start? OK, please begin.

Assessment Procedure
'Administer pre-set simulations and tests as required' refers to two possibilities:

1. In an industrial situation where processes cannot be interrupted, it may not be possible to observe a *natural performance* of the job. You may have to set up a situation which closely resembles or simulates the activity. After assessing the employee's performance, you should then ask questions on how the candidate would deal with the real situation eg, given time constraints, defective machinery, communication problems, etc. You may decide, having watched the candidate's performance, that there is not enough evidence that he or she can achieve the same performance in a real situation. In this case you can arrange another simulation to check consistency of performance or wait until a real opportunity presents itself.

2. You may need to use a pre-set test for example, one on measuring electrical currents. You might say 'I want you to measure the currents at these three points and state the results'. You then watch for correct use of the measuring device and the results obtained. Another example of a pre-set test is the use of written or oral questions that check a candidate's *underpinning knowledge*. The advantage of written set questions is that they lead to a high degree of standardization amongst assessors. There are clear Yes/No answers and the assessor's oral questioning technique is not a problem. If the job to be assessed is done in a noisy environment, any oral questions may well be best left for the beginning of the assessment or the end.

A workplace assessor needs good oral questioning skills. Questions should be used to check each performance stage and to find out if the candidate knows *why* he or she is carrying out the process: this helps to avoid a 'monkey see, monkey do' situation. The more complex the job, the more important it is to check knowledge and understanding. Questions that *lead* interfere with the reliability and validity of the assessment process. For example, 'Could you use the measuring device to measure the electric current. Make sure you move the switch all the way to the left', leads the candidate to the correct performance.

Other examples of invalid questioning are when you:

- ask a question and the candidate comes back with an answer which is unclear. You paraphrase: 'So what you are saying is...' and the candidate replies 'Yes';
- ask a question, the candidate gives half an answer and you complete it;
- ask an unclear or confusing question and the candidate comes back with an answer which is unclear because he or she is not clear about the question.

Feedback

Focus on behaviour that can be changed and relate this to future progress. At the end of the feedback session there should be a clear decision on the performance of the candidate. For example,

Joe I'm happy that you've met the required standard and will sign you off on this skill (or) Therefore Joe on the basis of the points I've made I will watch you perform this task again – next Wednesday at 2 o'clock.

The clearer a decision is, the less likely is the candidate to argue.

Benefits

The benefits of follow-up and observation at the job-site are that they:

- Involve managers and encourage the organization to support improved performance. The attention that you give to managers and employees makes them not only feel the training is important, but that *they* are important. In this way follow-up encourages support for training and visits to the job-site can include a marketing aspect as well as increase training's credibility.
- Provide additional help and support for participants after they have completed a training programme. In particular, follow-up helps participants apply their training to the job.
- Provide feedback on employee progress, on whether training standards have been achieved and on the effectiveness of the trainer and training. For the employee assessment also provides feedback on progress and an opportunity for certification of skills/achievements.
- Provide additional information on your participants' jobs; this information may indicate the need for course revisions or adjustments. It may also reveal additional needs and lead to requests for more training. In this way follow-ups often involve a re-diagnosis of needs or identification of additional needs which can be dealt with through training.

Finally, for the company follow-up and job observation can establish occupational standards, ensure the development of employee skills and can drive forward improvements in the quality of products or services.

Limitations

Follow-up interviews and observations at the job-site are expensive compared to other evaluation methods. Visits may be time-consuming as they involve travelling, meetings with managers and staff and time for your observations.

These visits are also demanding in terms of your interviewing and observation skills. If the interviews and observations are not handled diplomatically and as opportunities for collaboration, staff may become hostile and defensive.

Job observation and workplace assessment in particular require clear management understanding and support. Managers need to be able to integrate training and assessment into their operations and withstand complaints from people who need to be 'looked at again'. The credibility of the assessor and the assessment procedure is critical to any job training and assessment programme and assessors need to be trained and monitored.

Follow-up visits may sometimes show that the working environment does not support the training or improvement of performance. The organization's philosophy, goals, people, procedures, routines and even the physical layout back on the job may discourage employees from applying what they have learned. This environmental resistance plus resistance from past personal habits can create a powerful barrier to change. In this situation you might:

■ Try to reduce the resistance through your discussions with managers and supervisors.
■ Make sure that these barriers are faced during the training programme, and strategies for successful application of training are developed before participants return to the job. This is one of the reasons why needs assessment is so important before you develop training. It is also the rationale for including activities like case studies, role-plays, practice sessions and action planning in preparation for implementation back on the job.
■ Report the situation to your management. Training is concerned with improving the performance of individuals and organizations; obstacles to performance improvement need to be identified for management to take appropriate action.

Level 5: Business impact

The question here is, 'What has been the impact on the business of employees using these skills?' Evaluation of training's business impact is perhaps the most difficult and least common form of training evaluation. At this level trainers try to measure the effects of participants' job performance on the productivity or efficiency of their organizations. Obviously this level of evaluation is intimately bound to the Level 4 evaluation which provides evidence of the transfer of knowledge, skills and attitudes back to the job. If this individual transfer of training did not occur, obviously a Level 5 evaluation cannot show any results.

How it's done

In order to determine the impact of training at the organizational level, you can obtain data on areas such as:

- increases in productivity;
- improvements in the quality of products and reductions in 'scrap';
- reduced unit and operating costs;
- improved safety levels with fewer accidents and safety violations;
- higher levels of customer satisfaction, as shown by increased sales, reduction in returns, fewer complaints, etc.;
- reductions in employee turnover, absenteeism and employee grievances.

You can compare pre-training data to post-training data, or compare staff who participated in the training with a *control group* – a group with similar jobs and background, who did not participate in the training. If the relevant data are already routinely collected and recorded, data collection should not be expensive. However, creating a system specifically for collecting and interpreting data for training evaluation can be difficult, time-consuming and costly.

In addition to data collection on the impact of training, a Level 5 evaluation requires data on the total cost of training. You will need to collect information in the following areas:

- Personnel – the salaries and expenses of everyone involved in developing and conducting the training. Include the cost of the participants' time for the actual period of the training.
- Facilities – the cost of classrooms, laboratories, learning centres, etc.
- Equipment – the cost of computers, audio-visual equipment, etc.
- Course materials – computer software, participant manuals, videos, etc.
- Accommodation and travel – the expenses of the trainer(s) and participants.
- Meals and refreshments – the expenses of the trainer(s) and participants.

In order to arrive at the return on investment (ROI) you divide the financial value of the training by the total training cost. For example, after a training programme you might find an improvement in the quality of a product and a reduction in 'scrap'; quality improvement might then produce increased sales. To obtain the ROI percentage you compute the value of these improvements, divide by the cost of training, and multiply by 100. Any ROI value greater than 100 per cent represents a significant return on investment.

Benefits

Evaluation of training's business impact shows your commitment to supporting and serving the organization. It ties training in more closely to organizational goals and objectives and fits in with management rhetoric about training needing to be more 'business- and results-oriented'. As training is evaluated in terms of benefits to the organization, evidence from this type of evaluation can be used to support training in times of cutbacks.

Evaluation of training's business impact is also likely to reveal and highlight additional training needs with which management may want assistance.

Limitations

Many of the benefits from effective training are indirect and often intangible. For example, if managers and supervisors are trained to improve their communication with subordinates, we may have no idea how to measure the effect of these changes on the functioning of the company. Indeed unless the training is linked to quantifiable business outcomes, there is no reason for a Level 5 evaluation.

Increased morale, improvements in quality of work, improved safety, reduction in employee turnover and absenteeism, etc. can be observed and in some cases measured, but they may result from a variety of factors, not just training. Indeed, it is sometimes difficult to know how much an improvement may be due to a particular training programme and how much to other factors eg, changes in personnel, procedures, salaries, the overall economic environment. Moreover, by trying to show that training alone is responsible for improvements, you may alienate other departments and groups who might feel that their efforts are responsible for the improvement as well.

Many organizations and trainers ignore Level 5 evaluation. This is because the evaluation of organizational results can be time-consuming, fairly expensive and ultimately rather nebulous.

Evaluation strategy

Your evaluation strategy will depend on the importance of training evaluation to the following groups and factors.

Management

Is your management concerned about evaluation? Would additional or more accurate evaluation help you gain extra resources, or justify the resources you already have? As mentioned earlier, 'justification' is becoming increasingly important and you must be prepared to act if management concerns for 'quality' arise.

We all know of situations where a manager or supervisor has been on a course which was useful and as a result has sent his or her own people on that course. Conversely, we know of situations where one or two important people have criticized a course and this has had a disproportionate effect on management attitudes. In the latter situation, feedback forms and other evaluation tools become very important.

So, in relation to management we must not ignore or neglect the effects of informal evaluation. Informal grapevine feedback from other people can influence decisions as much as any data or reports we present. Good communication with management is vital and better informal communication with decisionmakers is needed if they are to learn the real value of our programmes.

Quality of the training programme

If your management, you and the clients are satisfied with your courses and they are generally agreed to fit the needs, there is not much justification for putting a lot of resources into evaluation. If you are revising a particular course however, you will need to evaluate the course as part of the revision needs survey. This again emphasizes the close relationship between evaluation and needs assessment.

Present training situation

This includes the resources – the time, manpower, expertise, money – available for evaluation. The issue arises as to whether these resources might be better used in some other training effort, for example the development of a new course and new materials.

Your clients

If they feel evaluation is important, they will be more willing to collaborate in an evaluation study and provide information and time. You may find also that evaluation is likely to uncover additional training needs and that 'quality' concerns and efforts are increasing the demand for training.

Evaluation Step	Evaluation Methods
1. Trainer(s) evaluate the training modules as each one is completed	Trainer checklist/dry-run
2. Participants record reactions after the course	Participant feedback form
3. Trainer(s) evaluate participants' learning	Written or performance tests
4. Trainer(s) follow-up at the job site	Interview, observation, workplace assessment
5. Trainer(s) evaluate the organizational effectiveness of training programme	Collect data on: • Training programmer graduates' performance • Increases in sales, quality, productivity, etc. • Reductions in complaints, errors, employee turnover, etc.

Figure 6.8 *Sample evaluation programme*

Most evaluation of training is done at Levels 1, 2, 3 and 4; the evaluation programme shown in Figure 6.8 covers the first four levels and offers a programme that is fairly easy to implement once you have developed the evaluation tools. In training magazines and books there is more talk of evaluation at the organization level (Level 5) but as Kirkpatrick (1987) comments: 'The evaluation of training programs in terms of "results" is progressing at a very slow rate'. Indeed if you evaluate training, try to make a good job of the first four levels before venturing to deal with the results and impact on the organization.

Finally a word of caution: avoid evaluating by any method unless you foresee the use to which the evaluation data will be put and judge that this usefulness makes the evaluation worthwhile.

Reporting the evaluation

Many of the points and suggestions made in Chapter 2 about the development and presentation of a needs survey report apply also to any evaluation report. The report should include:

■ Executive summary – probably the most important part of the report because management may read only this. The summary should set out to answer the 'Why', 'How', 'What', and 'What should we do?' questions that management will want answered.
■ Introduction and background – the situation that led to the evaluation.
■ Method(s) – how the evaluation was carried out and the reasons for the method or methods used.
■ Evaluation findings or results – numbered so that they can be reviewed and referred to more easily.
■ Discussion or analysis – including a discussion of the implications of the evaluation for the development of training and organizational improvement.
■ Recommendations – numbered so that they can be reviewed and referred to more easily.
■ Appendices – supporting documentation on the measurement instruments, statistical data, etc.

An evaluation study needs to take a constructive approach, collaborate with, and gain the support of the managers and staff of the organization involved. The long-term objective should be to build up a consulting relationship with the client organization and present evaluation as one of the services made available to the client.

Project Action Items: Evaluate a training programme

1. Considering the training programmes you are involved with, how could you in your organization improve the evaluation of:

- training programme development
- participant reactions after the programme
- participant learning during the programme
- participant performance on the job
- business impact

If you are not evaluating at one of these levels, how might you?

2. Consider a training programme that you know or are involved with. Using the table given below, estimate the cost of the programme.

TRAINING AREA	COST
Personnel – training staff and participants	
Facilities – classrooms, laboratories, learning centres, etc.	
Equipment – computers, audio-visual equipment, etc.	
Course materials – software, participant manuals, videos	
Travel – trainers and participants	
Accommodation – trainers and participants	
Meals and refreshments – trainers and participants	
TOTAL	

List what you consider are the benefits of the programme. Estimate, if you can, the financial value of these benefits.

References and further resources

Chapter 1

The Wheel of Learning is based upon models developed by David Kolb, University Associates in the US, and Charles Handy in Britain.

Dale, Edgar (1954) *Audio-visual Methods in teaching*, Dryden Press.

Fletcher, Shirley (1992) *Competence-Based Assessment Techniques,* Kogan Page, London.

Handy, Charles (1990) *The Age of Unreason, Arrow Books, London.*

Keller, John (1987) 'The systematic process of motivational design' in *Performance and Instruction* (November/December).

Knowles, Malcolm (1980) *The Modern Practice of Adult Education*, The Adult Education Company Cambridge, MA pp. 50, 56 and 234.

Kolb, David (1976) *Learning Style Inventory Technical Manual,*. McBer, Boston.

Maslow, Abraham (1970) *Motivation and Personality*, Harper and Row, London.

Senge, Peter (1990) *The Fifth Discipline*, Century Business, London.

Chapter 2

Knowles, Malcolm (1980) *The Modern Practice of Adult Education*, The Adult Education Co., Cambridge, MA.

Laird, Dugan (1985) *Approaches to Training and Development*, Addison-Wesley, Wokingham.

Mager, Robert F (1991) *Making Instruction Work*, Kogan Page, London.

Rosset, Allison (1987) *Training Needs Assessment*, Educational Technology Publications, New Jersey.

Zemke, Ron and Kramlington, Thomas (1982) *Figuring Things Out – A Trainer's guide to needs and task analysis*, Addison-Wesley, Wokingham.

Chapter 3

The annual *Developing Human Resources* is published by Pfeiffer and Co, University Associates, 85127 Production Avenue, San Diego, California 92121. Kogan Page produce One-Day Workshop Packages which can be ordered direct from Kogan Page, 120 Pentonville Road, London N1 9JN.

Mager, Robert F (1991) *Preparing Instructional Objectives*, Kogan Page, London.

Lego Man is described in Pfeiffer, J William (1972) *Annual Handbook for Group Facilitators*, University Associates, San Diego, CA.

Chapter 4

Pike, Robert (1990) *Creative Training Techniques*, Lakewood Publications, Minneapolis, MN.

Taylor, M (1988) *Planning for Video: A guide to making effective training videotapes*, Kogan Page, London.

Well-known suppliers of training videos include:

Longman Training, Longman House, Burnt Mill, Harlow, Essex CM20 2JE.

Video Arts Ltd, Dumbarton House, 68 Oxford Street, London W1N 9LA.

Chapter 5

The situational leadership approach is described by Paul Hersey and Kenneth H Blanchard in a series of books starting in 1982 with *Management of Organizational Behavior: Utilizing human resources*, Prentice Hall, New Jersey. The situational leadership course is used in management training courses around the world and is available from Blanchard Training and Development, 125 State Place, Escondido, CA 92029.

Chapter 6

Fletcher, Shirley (1992) *Competence-based Assessment Techniques*, Kogan Page, London.

Kirkpatrick, Donald L (1987) 'Evaluation' in *Training and Development Handbook* (3rd ed) McGraw-Hill, Maidenhead. Kirkpatrick's articles on evaluating training are from *Training and Development Journal*, American Society for Training and Development.

Robinson, Kenneth R (1988) *A Handbook of Training Management*, Kogan Page, London.

General resources for the trainer

The Training Directory is published annually by Kogan Page in association with the British Association for Commercial and Industrial Education (BACIE). The directory gives information on consultants, course providers, training centres and suppliers of training materials and equipment. The directory also provides information on the latest UK government training initiatives and the Training and Enterprise Councils.

Training and Development is published monthly by the Institute of Personnel Development, Marlow House, Institute Road, Marlow, Buckinghamshire SL7 1BN, England.

Training magazine is published monthly by Lakewood Publications, Lakewood Building, 50, Ninth St, Minneapolis, MN 55402, USA.

Training and Development Journal is published monthly by the American Society for Training and Development, 1640 King Street, Box 1443, Alexandria, VA 22313–2043, USA.

INDEX

cool 64
follow-up 195
hot 64
how to use 64–7
in needs assessment 56–9
induction needs 65
limitations 59
noise 64
preparation for 45–6, 65
structured 57
with customer 46–8
with prospective customer 45–6

job aids 41, 117–19
job observation 59–61, 197–201
benefits of using 60
how to use 67–72
limitations of 60–61
management understanding and
    support 201
job performance, evaluation 194–201

Keller, John 21, 22, 28, 33
KISS principle 42–3, 89, 155
knowledge objectives 84, 85
Knowles, Malcolm 28, 29, 34, 56
Kolb, David A. 26

Laird, Dugan 34, 38, 53, 57, 59
learning
activities involved 16
application 18–19
assessing 174–8
climate conducive to 150
comfortable environment 23–5
    training applications 24–5
control over content and activities
    29–30
    training applications 29–30
dealing with realistic problems 30–31
definitions 15–16
developments 15–17
focus on 162–3
principles of 19–37
process of 16–19
promotion in organizations 15–37
reviewing 174–8
stages of 18

learning cycle 18, 93
learning journals 192, 197
learning needs 25–7
training applications 27
learning styles 25–7, 103
dimensions of 26
love, affection and sense of belonging 21

Mager, Robert 34, 39, 81
management involvement 40–41
management report 48
management trainer 11
market pressures 10
market research 42
Maslow, Abraham H. 20, 22, 34
media presentation 91, 156–7
mentors 41
motivation 19–23
ARCS model 21, 22, 28, 33
definition 30
training applications 22

National Vocational Qualifications
    (NVQ) 35–6, 197
networking 44, 45
norm-referenced assessment 35

observation
structured 169–70
see also job observation
on-the-job trainer 11
on-the-job training 29
on-the-job training (OJT) 87
optional tasks 60
overhead transparencies (OHTs) 123–6
developing 123
preparation 125
production 124–5
use 125–6
overlearning 34

pair activities 163
pair exercise 150
participant involvement 31–2, 139–78
common problem situations 175–6
confirmation of arrangements 141
facilitating 161–73
introductions 149–50

SECOND EDITION

HOW TO DEVELOP AND PRESENT

STAFF TRAINING COURSES

'An excellent sound introduction to training . . . thoroughly recommended.' IT TRAINING

'This is an excellent book.' PERSONNEL MANAGEMENT

Every business or organization needs an effective and coherent staff training and development programme in order to make the best use of its most important resource – the people who work for it. Now in its second edition, this influential and bestselling book provides an in-depth consideration of all the issues involved in establishing a training programme, from assessing the needs of a particular group of employees to developing the training course, presenting it and evaluating its success afterwards.

Completely updated, and with new material covering topics such as competence-based training, job observation, task analysis, producing training videos and workplace assessment, **How to Develop and Present Staff Training Courses** is a practical handbook for all trainers, training programme developers and HRD personnel involved in the development or presentation of training courses and workshops. It considers such fundamental issues as:

- **How to promote learning**
- **How to assess staff needs**
- **How to develop a course**
- **How to develop and use training materials**
- **How to conduct a course**
- **How to follow up on and evaluate training.**

Thoughout the book, extensive use is made of job aids that can be used in training – diagrams, flowcharts, forms and checklists. A variety of training situations and examples is used to provide a practical step-by-step approach to course development and presentation.

The Author

Peter Sheal has worked in education and training for 20 years. Since 1981 he has worked in staff training and development for a major Middle East oil company as supervisor of staff development programmes. In this capacity he is responsible for developing and implementing training courses for teachers, trainers, on-the-job trainers, supervisory and management staff.

£18.95

ISBN 0-7494-1231-3

Kogan Page
120 Pentonville Road
London N1 9JN

NP
Published in the USA by
Nichols Publishing,
PO Box 6036,
East Brunswick,
New Jersey 08816

9 780749 412319